ONLY WORDS

CATHARINE A. MacKINNON

▼

ONLY *Words*

▼

HARVARD UNIVERSITY PRESS

Cambridge, Massachusetts

First Harvard University Press paperback edition, 1996

Designed by Marianne Perlak
Typeface is Adobe Minion

Library of Congress Cataloging-in-Publication Data

MacKinnon, Catharine A.
Only words / Catharine A. MacKinnon.
p. cm.
Includes bibliographical references and index.
ISBN 0-674-63933-2 (cloth)
ISBN 0-674-63934-0 (pbk.)
1. Freedom of speech—United States.
2. Equality before the law—United States.
3. Libel and slander—United States.
4. Racism in language.
5. Sexism in language—United States.
I. Title.
KF4772.M33   1993
342.73'085—dc20
[347.30285]

93-13600
CIP

In memory of Thomas I. Emerson

ACKNOWLEDGMENTS

Originally presented as the Christian Gauss Memorial Lectures in Criticism in April 1992 at Princeton University, these three discussions took their current form as a result of the instigation and inspiration of that forum. Later, the Columbia Legal Theory Workshop and, especially, Owen Fiss's Feminist Legal Theory class at Yale Law School provided supportive settings for their development and clarification. They have benefited greatly from the critical attention and acumen of Anne Simon, Sheila Kuehl, Susanne Baer, Karen E. Davis, Cass Sunstein, Kent Harvey, and Jeffrey Masson, discussions with Laurence Tribe, and over a decade of collaboration with Andrea Dworkin. Susanne Baer, Cheryl Leighty, and the ever resourceful Michigan Law Library provided research assistance of the highest quality.

CONTENTS

I

▼

DEFAMATION
AND
DISCRIMINATION

▼

I MAGINE that for hundreds of years your most formative traumas, your daily suffering and pain, the abuse
you live through, the terror you live with, are unspeak-
able—not the basis of literature. You grow up with your
father holding you down and covering your mouth so
another man can make a horrible searing pain between
your legs. When you are older, your husband ties you to
the bed and drips hot wax on your nipples and brings in
other men to watch and makes you smile through it.
Your doctor will not give you drugs he has addicted you
to unless you suck his penis.[1]

You cannot tell anyone. When you try to speak of
these things, you are told it did not happen, you imagined it, you wanted it, you enjoyed it. Books say this. No
books say what happened to you. Law says this. No law
imagines what happened to you, the way it happened.
You live your whole life surrounded by this cultural echo
of nothing where your screams and your words should
be.

In this thousand years of silence, the camera is in-
vented and pictures are made of you while these things

are being done. You hear the camera clicking or whirring as you are being hurt, keeping time to the rhythm of your pain. You always know that the pictures are out there somewhere, sold or traded or shown around or just kept in a drawer. In them, what was done to you is immortal. He has them; someone, anyone, has seen you there, that way. This is unbearable. What he felt as he watched you as he used you is always being done again and lived again and felt again through the pictures— your violation his arousal, your torture his pleasure. Watching you was how he got off doing it; with the pictures he can watch you and get off any time.[2]

Slowly, then suddenly, it dawns on you: maybe now I will be believed. You find a guarded way of bringing it up. Maybe the pictures are even evidence of rape.[3] You find that the pictures, far from making what happened undeniable, are sex, proof of your desire and your consent.[4] Those who use you through the pictures feel their own pleasure. They do not feel your pain as pain any more than those who watched as they hurt you to make the pictures felt it. The pictures, surrounded by a special halo of false secrecy and false taboo—false because they really are public and are not really against the rules— have become the authority on what happened to you, the literature of your experience, a sign for sex, sex itself. In a very real way, they have made sex *be* what it is to the people who use you and the pictures of you interchangeably. In this, the pictures are not so different from the words and drawings that came before, but your use for the camera gives the pictures a special credibility, a deep verisimilitude, an even stronger claim to truth, to being incontrovertibly about you, because they happened and there you are. And because you are needed for the pictures, the provider has yet another reason to use you over and over and over again.

Finally, somehow, you find other women. Their fathers, husbands, and doctors saw the pictures, liked them, and did the same things to them, things they had never done or said they wanted before. As these other women were held down, or tied up, or examined on the table, pictures like the pictures of you were talked about or pointed to: do what she did, enjoy it the way she enjoyed it. The same acts that were forced on you are forced on them; the same smile you were forced to smile, they must smile. There is, you find, a whole industry in buying and selling captive smiling women to make such pictures, acting as if they like it.

When any one of them tries to tell what happened, she is told it did not happen, she imagined it, she wanted it. Her no meant yes. The pictures prove it. See, she smiles. Besides, why fixate on the pictures, the little artifact, at most a symptom? Even if something wrong was *done* to you, how metaphysically obtuse can you be? The pictures *themselves* do nothing. They are an expression of ideas, a discussion, a debate, a discourse. How repressed and repressive can you be? They are constitutionally protected speech.

Putting to one side what this progression from life to law does to one's sense of reality, personal security, and place in the community, not to mention faith in the legal system, consider what it does to one's relation to expression: to language, speech, the world of thought and communication. You learn that language does not belong to you, that you cannot use it to say what you know, that knowledge is not what you learn from your life, that information is not made out of your experience. You learn that thinking about what happened to you does not count as "thinking," but doing it apparently does. You learn that your reality subsists somewhere beneath the socially real—totally exposed but invisible, screaming yet inaudible, thought about incessantly yet unthinkable, "expression" yet inexpressible, beyond words. You learn that speech is not what you say but what your abusers do to you.

Your relation to speech is like shouting at a movie. Somebody stop that man, you scream. The audience acts as though nothing has been said, keeps watching fixedly or turns slightly, embarrassed for you. The action on-screen continues as if nothing has been said. As the echo of your voice dies in your ears, you begin to doubt that you said anything. Soon your own experience is not real to you anymore, like a movie you watch but cannot stop. This is women's version of life imitating art: your life as the pornographer's text. To survive, you learn shame and how to cover it with sexual bravado, inefficacy and how to make it seductive, secrecy and the habit of not telling what you know until you forget it. You learn how to leave your body and create someone else who takes over when you cannot stand it any more. You develop a self who is ingratiating and obsequious and imitative and aggressively passive and silent—you learn, in a word, femininity.

I am asking you to imagine that women's reality is real—something of a leap of faith in a society saturated with pornography, not to mention an academy saturated with deconstruction.[5] In the early 1980s women spoke of this reality, in Virginia Woolf's words of many years before, "against the male flood":[6] they spoke of being sexually abused. Thirty-eight percent of women are sexually molested as girls; twenty-four percent of us are raped in our marriages. Nearly half are victims of rape or attempted rape at least once in our lives, many more than once, especially women of color, many involving multiple attackers, mostly men we know. Eighty-five percent of women who work outside the home are sexually harassed at some point by employers.[7] We do not yet know how many women are sexually harassed by their doctors or how many are bought and sold as sex—the one thing men will seemingly always pay for, even in a depressed economy.

A long time before the women's movement made this information available, in the absence of the words of sexually abused women, in the vacuum of this knowledge, in the silence of this speech, the question of pornography was framed and debated—its trenches dug, its moves choreographed, its voices rehearsed. Before the invention of the camera, which requires the direct use of real women; before the rise of a mammoth profitmaking industry of pictures and words acting as pimp; before women spoke out about sexual abuse and were heard, the question of the legal regulation of pornography was framed as a question of the freedom of expression of the pornographers and their consumers. The government's interest in censoring the expression of ideas about sex was opposed to publishers' right to express them and readers' right to read and think about them.

Frozen in the classic form of prior debates over censorship of political and artistic speech, the pornography debate thus became one of governmental authority threatening to suppress genius and dissent. There was some basis in reality for this division of sides. Under the law of obscenity, governments did try to suppress art and literature because it was sexual in content. This was before the camera required live fodder and usually resulted in the books' becoming bestsellers.

Once abused women are heard and—this is the real hitch—become real, women's silence can no longer be the context in which pornography and speech are analyzed. Into the symbiotic dance between left and right, between the men who love to hate each other, enters the captive woman, the terms of access to whom they have been fighting over.[8] Instead of the forces of darkness seeking to suppress what the forces of light are struggling to free, her captivity itself is made central and put in issue for the first time. This changes everything, or should. Before, each woman who said she was abused looked incredible or exceptional; now, the abuse appears deadeningly commonplace. Before, what was done to her was sex; now, it is sexual abuse. Before, she was sex; now, she is a human being gendered female—if anyone can figure out what that is.

In this new context, the expressive issues raised by pornography also change—or should. Protecting pornography means protecting sexual abuse *as* speech, at the same time that both pornography and its protection have deprived women *of* speech, especially speech against sexual abuse. There is a connection between the silence enforced on women, in which we are seen to love and choose our chains because they have been sexualized, and the noise of pornography that surrounds us, passing for discourse (ours, even) and parading under constitutional protection. The operative definition of censorship accordingly shifts from government silencing what powerless people say, to powerful people violating powerless people into silence and hiding behind state power to do it.

In the United States, pornography is protected by the state.[9] Conceptually, this protection relies centrally on putting it back into the context of the silence of violated women: from real abuse back to an "idea" or "viewpoint" on women and sex. In this de-realization of the subordination of women, this erasure of sexual abuse through which a technologically sophisticated traffic in women becomes a consumer choice of expressive content, abused women become a pornographer's "thought" or "emotion." This posture unites pornography's apologists from libertarian economist and judge Frank Easterbrook[10] to liberal philosopher-king Ronald Dworkin,[11] from conservative scholar and judge Richard Posner[12] to pornographers' lawyer Edward DeGrazia.[13]

In their approach, taken together, pornography falls presumptively into the legal category "speech" at the outset through being rendered in terms of "content," "message," "emotion," what it "says," its "viewpoint," its "ideas." Once the women abused in it and through it are elided this way, its artifact status as pictures and words gets it legal protection through a seemingly indelible categorical formalism that then must be negated for anything to be done.

In this approach, the approach of current law, pornography is essentially treated as defamation rather than as discrimination.[14] That is, it is conceived in terms of what it says, which is imagined more or less effective or harmful as someone then acts on it, rather than in terms of what it does. Fundamentally, in this view, a form of communication cannot, as such, *do* anything bad except offend. Offense is all in the head. Because the purveyor is protected in sending, and the consumer in receiving, the thought or feeling, the fact that an unintended bystander might have offended thoughts or unpleasant feelings is a mere externality, a cost we must pay for freedom. That the First Amendment protects this process of interchange—thought to thought, feeling to feeling—there is no doubt.

Within the confines of this approach, to say that pornography is an act against women is seen as metaphorical or magical, rhetorical or unreal, a literary hyperbole or propaganda device. On the assumption that words have only a referential relation to reality, pornography is defended as only words—even when it is pictures women had to be directly used to make, even when the means of writing are women's bodies, even when a woman is destroyed in order to say it or show it or because it was said or shown.

A theory of protected speech begins here: words express, hence are *presumed* "speech" in the protected sense. Pictures partake of the same level of expressive protection. But social life is full of words that are legally treated as the acts they constitute without so much as a whimper from the First Amendment. What becomes interesting is when the First Amendment frame is invoked and when it is not. *Saying* "kill" to a trained attack dog is only words. Yet it is not seen as expressing the viewpoint "I want you dead"—which it usually does, in fact, express. It is seen as performing an act tantamount to someone's destruction, like saying "ready, aim, fire" to a firing squad. Under bribery statutes, saying the word "aye" in a legislative vote triggers a crime that can consist entirely of what people say. So does price-fixing under the antitrust laws. "Raise your goddamn fares twenty percent, I'll raise mine the next morning" is not protected speech; it is attempted joint monopolization, a "highly verbal crime." In this case, conviction nicely disproved the defendant's view, expressed in the same conversation, that "we can talk about any goddamn thing we want to talk about."[15]

Along with other mere words like "not guilty" and "I do," such words are uniformly treated as the institutions and practices they constitute, rather than as expressions of the ideas they embody or further. They are not seen as saying anything (although they do) but as doing something. No one confuses discussing them with doing them, for instance discussing a verdict of "guilty" with a jury's passing a verdict of "guilty." Nobody takes an appeal of a guilty verdict as censorship of the jury. Such words are not considered "speech" at all.

Social inequality is substantially created and enforced—that is, *done*—through words and images. Social hierarchy cannot and does not exist without being embodied in meanings and expressed in communications. A sign *saying* "White Only"[16] is only words, but it is not legally seen as expressing the viewpoint "we do not want Black people in this store," or as dissenting from the policy view that both Blacks and whites must be served, or even as hate speech, the restriction of which would need to be debated in First Amendment terms. It is seen as the act of segregation that it is, like "Juden nicht erwünscht!"[17] Segregation cannot happen without someone *saying* "get out" or "you don't belong here" at some point. Elevation and denigration are all accomplished through meaningful symbols and communicative acts in which saying it is doing it.

Words unproblematically treated as acts in the inequality context include "you're fired," "help wanted—male," "sleep with me and I'll give you an A," "fuck me or you're fired," "walk more femininely, talk more femininely, dress more femininely, wear makeup, have your hair styled, and wear jewelry," and "it was essential that the understudy to my Administrative Assistant be a man."[18] These statements are discriminatory acts and are legally seen as such. Statements like them can also evidence discrimination or show that patterns of inequality are motivated by discriminatory animus. They can constitute actionable discriminatory acts in themselves or legally transform otherwise nonsuspect acts into bias-motivated ones. Whatever damage is done through such words is done not only through their context but through their content, in the sense that if they did not contain what they contain, and convey the meanings and feelings and thoughts they convey, they would not evidence or actualize the discrimination that they do.

Pornography, by contrast, has been legally framed as a vehicle for the expression of ideas. The Supreme Court of Minnesota recently observed of some pornography before it that "even the most liberal construction would be strained to find an 'idea' in it," limited as it was to "who wants what, where, when, how, how much, and how often."[19] Even this criticism dignifies the pornography. The *idea of* who wants what, where, and when sexually can be expressed without violating anyone and without getting anyone raped. There are many ways to say what pornography says, in the sense of its content.

But nothing else does what pornography does. The question becomes, do the pornographers—saying they are only saying what it says—have a speech right to do what only it does?

What pornography does, it does in the real world, not only in the mind. As an initial matter, it should be observed that it is the pornography industry, not the ideas in the materials, that forces, threatens, blackmails, pressures, tricks, and cajoles women into sex for pictures. In pornography, women are gang raped so they can be filmed. They are not gang raped by the idea of a gang rape. It is for pornography, and not by the ideas in it, that women are hurt and penetrated, tied and gagged, undressed and genitally spread and sprayed with lacquer and water so sex pictures can be made. Only for pornography are women killed to make a sex movie, and it is not the idea of a sex killing that kills them. It is unnecessary to do any of these things to express, as ideas, the ideas pornography expresses. It *is* essential to do them to make pornography. Similarly, on the consumption end, it is not the ideas in pornography that assault women: men do, men who are made, changed, and impelled by it. Pornography does not leap off the shelf and assault women. Women could, in theory, walk safely past whole warehouses full of it, quietly resting in its jackets. It is what it takes to make it and what happens through its use that are the problem.

Empirically, of all two-dimensional forms of sex, it is only pornography, not its ideas as such, that gives men erections that support aggression against women in particular. Put another way, an erection is neither a thought nor a feeling, but a behavior. It is only pornography that rapists use to select whom they rape and to get up for their rapes. This is not because they are persuaded by its ideas or even inflamed by its emotions, or because it is so conceptually or emotionally compelling, but because they are sexually habituated to its kick, a process that is largely unconscious and works as primitive conditioning, with pictures and words as sexual stimuli. Pornography consumers are not consuming an idea any more than eating a loaf of bread is consuming the ideas on its wrapper or the ideas in its recipe.

This is not to object to primitiveness or sensuality or subtlety or habituation in communication. Speech conveys more than its literal meaning, and its undertones and nuances must be protected. It is to question the extent to which the First Amendment protects unconscious mental intrusion and physical manipulation, even by pictures and words, particularly when the results are further acted out through aggression and other discrimination.[20] It is also to observe that pornography does not engage the conscious mind in the chosen way the model of "content," in terms of which it is largely defended, envisions and requires. In the words of Judge Easterbrook, describing this dynamic, pornography "does not persuade people so much as change them."[21]

Pornography is masturbation material.[22] It is used as sex. It therefore is sex. Men know this. In the centuries before pornography was made into an "idea" worthy of First Amendment protection, men amused themselves and excused their sexual practices by observing that the penis is not an organ of thought. Aristotle said, "it is impossible to think about anything while absorbed [in the pleasures of sex.]"[23] The Yiddish equivalent translates roughly as "a stiff prick turns the mind to shit."[24] The common point is that having sex is antithetical to thinking. It would not have occurred to them that having sex *is* thinking.

With pornography, men masturbate to women being exposed, humiliated, violated, degraded, mutilated, dismembered, bound, gagged, tortured, and killed. In the visual materials, they experience this *being done* by watching it *being done*. What is real here is not that the materials are pictures, but that they are part of a sex act. The women are in two dimensions, but the men have sex with them in their own three-dimensional bodies, not in their minds alone. Men come doing this. This, too, is a behavior, not a thought or an argument. It is not ideas they are ejaculating over. Try arguing with an orgasm sometime. You will find you are no match for the sexual access and power the materials provide.

The fact that this experience is sexual does not erupt *sui generis* from pornography all by itself, any more than the experience of access and power in rape or child abuse or sexual harassment or sexual murder is sexual in isolation. There is no such thing as pornography, or any social occurrence, all by itself. But, of these, it is only pornography of which it is said that the experience is not one of access and power but one of thought; only of pornography that it is said that unless you can show what it and it alone does, you cannot do anything about it; and only pornography that is protected as a constitutional right. The fact that pornography, like rape, has deep and broad social roots and cultural groundings makes it more rather than less active, galvanizing and damaging.

One consumer of rape pornography and snuff films recently made this point as only an honest perpetrator can: "I can remember when I get horny from looking at girly books and watching girly shows that I would want to go rape somebody. Every time I would jack off before I come I would be thinking of rape and the women I had raped and remembering how exciting it was. The pain on their faces. The thrill, the excitement."[25] This, presumably, is what the court that recently protected pornography as speech meant when it said that its effects depend upon "mental intermediation."[26] See, he was watching, wanting, thinking, remembering, feeling. He was also receiving the death penalty for murdering a young woman named Laura after raping her, having vaginal and anal intercourse with her corpse, and chewing on several parts of her body.

Sooner or later, in one way or another, the consumers want to live out the pornography further in three dimensions. Sooner or later, in one way or another, they do. *It* makes them want to; when they believe they can, when they feel they can get away with it, *they* do. Depending upon their chosen sphere of operation, they may use whatever power they have to keep the world a pornographic place so they can continue to get hard from everyday life. As pornography consumers, teachers may become epistemically incapable of seeing their women students as their potential equals and unconsciously teach about rape from the viewpoint of the accused. Doctors may molest anesthetized women, enjoy watching and inflicting pain during childbirth, and use pornography to teach sex education in medical school. Some consumers write on bathroom walls. Some undoubtedly write judicial opinions.[27]

Some pornography consumers presumably serve on juries, sit on the Senate Judiciary Committee, answer police calls reporting domestic violence, edit media accounts of child sexual abuse, and produce mainstream films. Some make wives and daughters and clients and students and prostitutes look at it and do what is in it. Some sexually harass their employees and clients, molest their daughters, batter their wives, and use prostitutes—with pornography present and integral to the acts. Some gang rape women in fraternities and at rest stops on highways, holding up the pornography and reading it aloud and mimicking it. Some become serial rapists and sex murderers—using and making pornography is inextricable to these acts—either freelancing or in sex packs known variously as sex rings, organized crime, religious cults, or white supremacist organizations. Some make pornography for their own use and as a sex act in itself, or in order to make money and support the group's habit.[28]

This does not presume that all pornography is made through abuse or rely on the fact that some pornography is made through coercion as a legal basis for restricting all of it.[29] Empirically, all pornography is made under conditions of inequality based on sex, overwhelmingly by poor, desperate, homeless, pimped women who were sexually abused as children. The industry's profits exploit, and are an incentive to maintain, these conditions. These conditions constrain choice rather than offering freedom. They are *what it takes* to make women do what is in even the pornography that shows no overt violence.

I have come to think that there is a connection between these conditions of production and the force that is so often needed to make other women perform the sex that consumers come to want as a result of viewing it. In other words, if it took these forms of force to make a woman do what was needed to make the materials, might it not take the same or other forms of force to get other women to do what is in it? Isn't there, then, an obvious link between the apparent need to coerce some women to perform for pornography and the coercion of other women as a result of its consumption? If a woman had to be coerced to make *Deep Throat*, doesn't that suggest that *Deep Throat* is dangerous to all women anywhere near a man who wants to do what he saw in it?[30]

Pornography contains ideas, like any other social practice. But the way it works is not as a thought or through its ideas as such, at least not in the way thoughts and ideas are protected as speech. Its place in abuse requires understanding it more in active than in passive terms, as constructing and performative[31] rather than as merely referential or connotative.

The message of these materials, and there is one, as there is to all conscious activity, is "get her," pointing at all women, to the perpetrators' benefit of ten billion dollars a year and counting. This message is addressed directly to the penis, delivered through an erection, and taken out on women in the real world. The content of this message is not unique to pornography. It is the function of pornography in effectuating it that is unique. Put another way, if there is anything that only pornography can say, that is exactly the measure of the harm that only pornography can do. Suppose the consumer could not get in any other way the feeling he gets from watching a woman actually be murdered. What is more protected, his sensation or her life? Should it matter if the murder is artistically presented? Shall we now balance away women's lesser entitlements—not to be raped, dehumanized, molested, invaded, and sold? Do the consequences for many women of doing this to some women, for mass marketing, weigh in this calculus? How many women's bodies have to stack up here even to register against male profit and pleasure presented as First Amendment principle?

On the basis of its reality, Andrea Dworkin and I have proposed a law against pornography that defines it as graphic sexually explicit materials that subordinate women through pictures or words.[32] This definition describes what is there, that is, what must be there for the materials to work as sex and to promote sexual abuse across a broad spectrum of consumers. This definition includes the harm of what pornography says—its function as defamation or hate speech—but defines it and it alone in terms of what it does—its role as subordination, as sex discrimination, including what it does through what it says. This definition is coterminous with the industry, from *Playboy,* in which women are objectified and presented dehumanized as sexual objects or things for use; through the torture of women and the sexualization of racism and the fetishization of women's body parts; to snuff films, in which actual murder is the ultimate sexual act, the reduction to the thing form of a human being and the silence of women literal and complete. Such material combines the graphic sexually explicit—graphically showing explicit sex—with activities like hurting, degrading, violating, and humiliating, that is, actively subordinating, treating unequally, as less than human, on the basis of sex. Pornography is not restricted here because of what it says. It is restricted through what it does. Neither is it protected because it says something, given what it does.

Now, in First Amendment terms, what is "content"— the "what it says" element—here?[33] We are told by the Supreme Court that we cannot restrict speech *because* of what it says, but all restricted expression says something. Most recently, we have been told that obscenity and child pornography are content that can be regulated although what distinguishes child pornography is not its "particular literary theme."[34] In other words, it has a message, but it does not do its harm through that message. So what, exactly, are the children who are hurt through the use of the materials hurt by?[35]

Suppose that the sexually explicit has a content element: it contains a penis ramming into a vagina. Does that mean that a picture of this conveys the idea of a penis ramming into a vagina, or does the viewer see and experience a penis ramming into a vagina? If a man watches a penis ram into a vagina live, in the flesh, do we say he is watching the idea of a penis ramming into a vagina? How is the visual pornography different? When he then goes and rams his penis into a woman's vagina, is that because he has an idea, or because he has an erection? I am not saying his head is not attached to his body; I am saying his body is attached to his head.

The ideas pornography conveys, construed as "ideas" in the First Amendment sense, are the same as those in mainstream misogyny: male authority in a naturalized gender hierarchy, male possession of an objectified other. In this form, they do not make men hard. The erections and ejaculations come from providing a physical reality for sexual use, which is what pornography does. Pornography is often more sexually compelling than the realities it presents, more sexually real than reality. When the pimp does his job right, he has the woman exactly where the consumers want her. In the ultimate male bond, that between pimp and john, the trick is given the sense of absolute control, total access, power to take combined with the illusion that it is a fantasy, when the one who actually has that power is the pimp. For the consumer, the mediation provides the element of remove requisite for deniability. Pornography thus offers both types of generic sex: for those who want to wallow in filth without getting their hands dirty and for those who want to violate the pure and get only their hands wet.

None of this starts or stops as a thought or feeling. Pornography does not simply express or interpret experience; it substitutes for it. Beyond bringing a message from reality, it stands in for reality; it is existentially being there. This does not mean that there is no spin on the experience—far from it. To make visual pornography, and to live up to its imperatives, the world, namely women, must do what the pornographers want to "say." Pornography brings its conditions of production to the consumer: sexual dominance. As Creel Froman puts it, subordination is "doing someone else's language."[36] Pornography makes the world a pornographic place through its making and use, establishing what women are said to exist as, are seen as, are treated as, constructing the social reality of what a woman is and can be in terms of what can be done to her, and what a man is in terms of doing it.

As society becomes saturated with pornography, what makes for sexual arousal, and the nature of sex itself in terms of the place of speech in it, change. What was words and pictures becomes, through masturbation, sex itself. As the industry expands, this becomes more and more the generic experience of sex, the woman in pornography becoming more and more the lived archetype for women's sexuality in men's, hence women's, experience. In other words, as the human becomes thing and the mutual becomes one-sided and the given becomes stolen and sold, objectification comes to define femininity, and one-sidedness comes to define mutuality, and force comes to define consent as pictures and words become the forms of possession and use through which women are actually possessed and used. In pornography, pictures and words are sex. At the same time, in the world pornography creates, sex is pictures and words. As sex becomes speech, speech becomes sex.

The denial that pornography is a real force comes in the guise of many mediating constructions. At most, it is said, pornography reflects or depicts or describes or represents subordination that happens elsewhere. The most common denial is that pornography is "fantasy." Meaning it is unreal, or only an internal reality. For whom? The women in it may dissociate to survive, but it *is* happening to their bodies. The pornographer regularly uses the women personally and does not stop his business at fantasizing. The consumer masturbates to it, replays it in his head and onto the bodies of women he encounters or has sex with, lives it out on the women and children around him. Are the victims of snuff films fantasized to death?

Another common evasion is that pornography is "simulated." What can this mean? It always reminds me of calling rape with a bottle "artificial rape."[37] In pornography, the penis is shown ramming up into the woman over and over; this is because it actually was rammed up into the woman over and over. In mainstream media, violence is done through special effects; in pornography, women shown being beaten and tortured report being beaten and tortured. Sometimes "simulated" seems to mean that the rapes are not really rapes but are part of the story, so the woman's refusal and resistance are acting. If it is acting, why does it matter what the actress is really feeling? We are told unendingly that the women in pornography are *really* enjoying themselves (but it's simulated?). Is the man's erection on screen "simulated" too? Is he "acting" too?

No pornography is "real" sex in the sense of shared intimacy; this may make it a lie, but it does not make it "simulated." Nor is it real in the sense that it happened as it appears. To look real to an observing camera, the sex acts have to be twisted open, stopped and restarted, positioned and repositioned, the come shot often executed by another actor entirely. The women regularly take drugs to get through it. This is not to say that none of this happens in sex that is not for pornography; rather that, as a defense of pornography, this sounds more like an indictment of sex.

One wonders why it is not said that the pleasure is simulated and the rape is real, rather than the other way around. The answer is that the consumer's pleasure requires that the scenario conform to the male rape fantasy, which requires him to abuse her and her to like it. Paying the woman to appear to resist and then surrender does not make the sex consensual; it makes pornography an arm of prostitution. The sex is not chosen for the sex. Money is the medium of force and provides the cover of consent.

The most elite denial of the harm is the one that holds that pornography is "representation," when a representation is a nonreality. Actual rape arranges reality; ritual torture frames and presents it. Does that make them "representations," and so not rape and torture? Is a rape a representation of a rape if someone is watching it? When is the rapist *not* watching it? Taking photographs is part of the ritual of some abusive sex, an act of taking, the possession involved. So is watching while doing it and watching the pictures later. The photos are trophies; looking at the photos is fetishism. Is nude dancing a "representation" of eroticism or is it eroticism, meaning a sex act? How is a live sex show different? In terms of what the men are doing sexually, an audience watching a gang rape in a movie is no different from an audience watching a gang rape that is reenacting a gang rape from a movie, or an audience watching any gang rape.

To say that pornography is categorically or functionally representation rather than sex simply creates a distanced world we can say is not the real world, a world that mixes reality with unreality, art and literature with everything else, as if life does not do the same thing. The effect is to license whatever is done there, creating a special aura of privilege and demarcating a sphere of protected freedom, no matter who is hurt. In this approach, there is no way to prohibit rape if pornography is protected. If, by contrast, representation *is* reality, as other theorists argue, then pornography is no less an act than the rape and torture it represents.[38]

At stake in constructing pornography as "speech" is gaining constitutional protection for doing what pornography *does:* subordinating women through sex. This is not content as such, nor is it wholly other than content. Segregation is not the content of "help wanted— male" employment advertisements, nor is the harm of the segregation done without regard to the content of the ad. It is its function. Law's proper concern here is not with what speech says, but with what it does.[39] The meaning *of* pornography in the sense of interpretation may be an interesting problem, but it is not this one. This problem is its meaning *for* women: what it does in and to our lives.

I am not saying that pornography is conduct and therefore not speech, or that it does things and therefore says nothing and is without meaning, or that all its harms are noncontent harms. In society, nothing is without meaning. Nothing has no content. Society is made of words, whose meanings the powerful control, or try to. At a certain point, when those who are hurt by them become real, some words are recognized as the acts that they are. Converging with this point from the action side, nothing that happens in society lacks ideas or says nothing, including rape and torture and sexual murder. This presumably does not make rape and murder protected expression, but, other than by simplistic categorization, speech theory never says why not. Similarly, every act of discrimination is done because of group membership, such as on the basis of sex or race or both, meaning done either with that conscious thought, perception, knowledge, or consequence. Indeed, discriminatory intent, a mental state, is required to prove discrimination under the Fourteenth Amendment.[40] Does this "thought" make all that discrimination "speech"?

It is not new to observe that while the doctrinal distinction between speech and action is on one level obvious, on another level it makes little sense. In social inequality, it makes almost none. Discrimination does not divide into acts on one side and speech on the other. Speech acts. It makes no sense from the action side either. Acts speak. In the context of social inequality, so-called speech can be an exercise of power which constructs the social reality in which people live, from objectification to genocide. The words and images are either direct incidents of such acts, such as making pornography or requiring Jews to wear yellow stars, or are connected to them, whether immediately, linearly, and directly, or in more complicated and extended ways.

Together with all its material supports, authoritatively *saying* someone is inferior is largely how structures of status and differential treatment are demarcated and actualized. Words and images are how people are placed in hierarchies, how social stratification is made to seem inevitable and right, how feelings of inferiority and superiority are engendered, and how indifference to violence against those on the bottom is rationalized and normalized.[41] Social supremacy is made, inside and between people, through making meanings. To unmake it, these meanings and their technologies have to be unmade.

A recent Supreme Court decision on nude dancing provides an example of the inextricability of expression with action in an unrecognized sex inequality setting. Chief Justice Rehnquist wrote, for the Court, that nude dancing can be regulated without violating the First Amendment because one can *say* the same thing by dancing in pasties and a G-string.[42] No issues of women's inequality to men were raised in all the pondering of the First Amendment, although the dancers who were the parties to the case could not have been clearer that *they* were not expressing anything.[43] In previous cases like this, no one has ever said what shoving dollar bills up women's vaginas expresses.[44] As a result, the fact that the accessibility and exploitation of women through their use as sex is at once being said *and done* through presenting women dancing nude is not confronted. That women's inequality is simultaneously being expressed and exploited is never mentioned. Given the role of access to women's genitals in gender inequality, dancing in a G-string raises similar "themes" and does similar harms, but neither says nor does exactly the same thing.

Justice Souter, in a separate concurrence, got closer to reality when he said that nude dancing could be regulated because it is accompanied by rape and prostitution.[45] These harms are exactly what is made worse by the difference between dancing in a G-string and pasties, and dancing in the nude. Yet he did not see that these harms are inextricable from, and occur exactly through, what nude dancing *expresses*. Unlike the majority, Justice Souter said that dancing in a G-string does not express the same "erotic message"[46] as nude dancing. In other words, men are measurably more turned on by seeing women expose their sexual parts entirely to public view than almost entirely. Nobody said that expressing eroticism is speech-think for engaging in public sex. Justice Souter did say that the feeling nude dancing expresses "is eroticism."[47] To express eroticism is to engage in eroticism, meaning to perform a sex act. To say it is to do it, and to do it is to say it. It is also to do the harm of it and to exacerbate harms surrounding it. In this context, unrecognized by law, it is to practice sex inequality as well as to express it.

The legal treatment of crossburning in another recent Supreme Court opinion provides yet another example of the incoherence of distinguishing speech from conduct in the inequality context. Crossburning is nothing but an act, yet it is pure expression, doing the harm it does solely through the message it conveys. Nobody weeps for the charred wood. By symbolically invoking the entire violent history of the Ku Klux Klan, it *says,* "Blacks get out," thus engaging in terrorism and effectuating segregation. It carries the message of historic white indifference both to this message and to the imminent death for which it stands. Segregating transportation expressed (at a minimum) the view that African-Americans should ride separately from whites; it was not seen to raise thorny issues of symbolic expression. Ads for segregated housing are only words, yet they are widely prohibited outright as acts of segregation.[48]

Like pornography, crossburning is seen by the Supreme Court to raise crucial expressive issues. Its function as an enforcer of segregation, instigator of lynch mobs, instiller of terror, and emblem of official impunity is transmuted into a discussion of specific "disfavored subjects."[49] The burning cross is the discussion. The "subject" is race—discriminating on the basis of it, that is. The bland indifference to reality is underlined by the lack of a single mention of the Ku Klux Klan. Recognizing the content communicated, Justice Stevens nonetheless characterized the crossburning as "nothing more than a crude form of physical intimidation."[50]

In this country, nothing has at once expressed racial hatred and effectuated racial subordination more effectively than the murder and hanging of a mutilated body, usually of a Black man. I guess this makes Black male bodies the subject of the discussion. Lynching expresses a clear point of view.[51] Photographs were sometimes taken of the body and sold, to extend its message and the pleasure of viewing it.[52] More discussion. Are these acts inexpressive and contentless? Are the pictures protected expression? Is a Black man's death made unreal by being photographed the way women's subordination is?[53] Suppose lynchings were done to make pictures of lynchings. Should their racist content protect them as political speech, since they do their harm through conveying a political ideology? Is *bigoted* incitement to murder closer to protected speech than plain old incitement to murder?[54] Does the lynching itself raise speech issues, since it is animated by a racist ideology? If the lynching includes rape, is it, too, potentially speech? A categorical no will not do here. Why, consistent with existing speech theory, are these activities not expressive? If expressive, why not protected?

Consider snuff pornography, in which women or children are killed to make a sex film. This is a film of a sexual murder in the process of being committed. Doing the murder is sex for those who do it. The climax is the moment of death. The intended consumer has a sexual experience watching it. Those who kill as and for sex are having sex through the murder; those who watch the film are having sex through watching the murder. A snuff film is not a discussion of the idea of sexual murder any more than the acts being filmed are. The film is not "about" sexual murder; it sexualizes murder. Is your first concern what a snuff film *says* about women and sex or what it does? Now, why is rape different?

Child pornography is exclusively a medium of pictures and words. The Supreme Court has referred to it as "pure speech."[55] Civil libertarians and publishers argued to protect it as such.[56] Child pornography conveys very effectively the idea that children enjoy having sex with adults, the feeling that this is liberating for the child. Yet child pornography is prohibited as child abuse, based on the use of children to make it.[57] A recent Supreme Court case in passing extended this recognition of harm to other children downstream who are made to see and imitate the pictures.[58] Possessing and distributing such pictures is punishable by imprisonment consistent with the First Amendment, despite the fact that private reading is thereby restricted. Harm like this may be what the Supreme Court left itself open to recognizing when it said, in guaranteeing the right to possess obscenity in private, that "compelling reasons may exist for overriding the right of the individual to possess" the prohibited materials.[59]

The point here is that sex pictures are legally considered sex acts, based on what, in my terms, is abuse due to the fact of inequality between children and adults. For seeing the pictures as tantamount to acts, how, other than that sexuality socially defines women, is inequality among adults different?

Now compare the lynching photograph and the snuff film with a *Penthouse* spread of December 1984 in which Asian women are trussed and hung.[60] One bound between her legs with a thick rope appears to be a child. All three express ideology. All had to be done to be made. All presumably convey something as well as provide entertainment. If used at work, this spread would create a hostile unequal working environment actionable under federal sex discrimination law.[61] But there is no law against a hostile unequal living environment, so everywhere else it is protected speech.

Not long after this issue of *Penthouse* appeared, a little Asian girl was found strung up and sexually molested in

North Carolina, dead.[62] The murderer said he spent much of the day of the murder in an adult bookstore. Suppose he consumed the *Penthouse* and then went and killed the little girl. Such linear causality, an obsession of pornography's defenders, is not all that rare or difficult to prove. It is only one effect of pornography, but when one *has* that effect, is restricting those pictures "thought control,"[63] the judicial epithet used to invalidate our law against pornography? Would the girl's death be what *Penthouse* "said"? If she was killed because of its "content," should it be protected?[64]

Should it matter: the evidence of the harm of such materials—from testimony of victims (called evidence, not anecdote, in court) to laboratory studies in which variables and predisposed men are controlled for, to social studies in which social reality is captured in all its messiness—shows that these materials change attitudes and impel behaviors in ways that are unique in their extent and devastating in their consequences. In human society, where no one does not live, the physical response to pornography is nearly a universal conditioned male reaction, whether they like or agree with what the materials say or not. There is a lot wider variation in men's conscious attitudes toward pornography than there is in their sexual responses to it.

There is no evidence that pornography does no harm; not even courts equivocate over its carnage anymore.[65]

The new insult is that the potency of pornography *as idea* is said to be proven by the harm it does, so it must be protected as speech.[66] Having made real harm into the idea of harm, discrimination into defamation, courts tell us in essence that to the extent materials are defamatory, meaning they contain defamatory ideas, they are protected, even as they discriminate against women from objectification to murder.

"Every idea is an incitement," said Justice Holmes in a famous dissent in an early case on freedom of speech.[67] Whether or not this is true to the same degree for every idea, it has come to mean that every incitement to action that has an idea behind it—especially a big idea, and misogyny is a very big idea—is to that degree First Amendment protected territory. This doctrine was originally created to protect from suppression the speech of communists, thought by some to threaten the security of the U.S. government. This experience is the crucible of the "speech" doctrine, its formative trauma, the evil of suppression of dissent that First Amendment law, through coming to terms with this debacle, has been designed to avoid. This is where we got the idea that we must protect ideas regardless of the mischief they do in the world, where the First Amendment got its operative idea of what an "idea" is.

Applying this paradigm for political speech to pornography requires placing, by analogy, sexually abused women relative to their abusers, in a position of power comparable to that of the U.S. government relative to those who advocated its overthrow. This is bizarre, given that risk of harm is the issue. Women are far more likely to be harmed through pornography than the U.S. government is to be overthrown by communists. Putting the pornographers in the posture of the excluded underdog, like communists, plays on the deep free speech tradition against laws that restrict criticizing the government. Need it be said, women are not the government? Pornography has to be done to women to be made; no government has to be overthrown to make communist speech. It is also interesting that whether or not forced sex is a good idea—pornography's so-called viewpoint on the subordination of women—is not supposed to be debatable to the same degree as is the organization of the economy. In theory, we have criminal laws against sexual abuse. We even have laws mandating sex equality.

Yet the First Amendment orthodoxy that came out of the communist cases is reflexively applied to pornography: if it is words and pictures, it expresses ideas. It *does* nothing. The only power to be feared as real is that of the government in restricting it. The speech is impotent. The analogy to communism has the realities reversed. Not only is pornography more than mere words, while the words of communism *are* only words. The power of pornography is more like the power of the state.[68] It is backed by power at least as great, at least as unchecked, and at least as legitimated. At this point, indeed, its power *is* the power of the state. State power protects it, silencing those who are hurt by it and making sure they can do nothing about it.

Law is only words. It has content, yet we do not analyze law as the mere expression of ideas. When we object to a law—say, one that restricts speech—we do not say we are offended by it. We are scared or threatened or endangered by it. We look to the consequences of the law's enforcement as an accomplished fact and to the utterance of legal words as tantamount to imposing their reality. This becomes too obvious to mention not only because the First Amendment does not protect government speech but because law is backed by power, so its words are seen as acts. But so is pornography: the power of men over women,[69] expressed through unequal sex, sanctioned both through and prior to state power. It makes no more sense to treat pornography as mere abstraction and representation than it does to treat law as simulation or fantasy. No one has suggested that our legal definition of pornography does what the pornography it describes in words does; nor that, if enacted in law, our ordinance would be only words.

As Andrea Dworkin has said, "pornography is the law for women."[70] Like law, pornography does what it says. That pornography is reality is what silenced women have not been permitted to *say* for hundreds of years. Failing to face this in its simplicity leaves one defending abstraction at the cost of principle, obscuring this emergency because it is not like other emergencies, defending an idea of an "idea" while a practice of sexual abuse becomes a constitutional right. Until we face this, we will be left where Andrea Dworkin recognizes we are left at the end of *Intercourse*:[71] with a violated child alone on the bed—this one wondering if she is lucky to be alive.

II

▼

RACIAL

AND

SEXUAL

HARASSMENT

I F E V E R words have been understood as acts, it has been when they are sexual harassment. For fifteen years, unremitting pressure for dates, unwelcome sexual comments, authoritative offers to exchange sex for benefits, and environments permeated with sexual vilification and abuse have been legally actionable in employment and education. Only words—yet they have not been seen as conveying ideas, although, like all social practices, they do: ideas like what men think of women, what men want to do to women, what women should do for men, where women belong. Sexualized racism and visual pornography have been integral to sexual harassment all along. In a not uncommon example, a Black woman worker was shown "a pornographic photograph depicting an interracial act of sodomy" by a white male co-worker who "told her that the photograph showed the 'talent' of a black woman" and "stated that she was hired for the purpose indicated in the photograph."[1]

Until recently, sexual harassment has never been imagined to raise expressive concerns, although all sexual harassment is words, pictures, meaningful acts and gestures.

45

Yet it has been legally understood in terms of what it does: discriminate on the basis of sex. Unwelcome sex talk is an unwelcome sex act. When threatening, severe, or pervasive enough, it works to exclude and segregate and denigrate and subordinate and dehumanize, violating human dignity and denying equality of opportunity. The First Amendment has not come up, even in a case in which a court issued an injunction prohibiting *saying* things like "Did you get any over the weekend?"[2] First Amendment issues have not often been raised against racial harassment claims either, even one in which the court found that the law requires employers to "take prompt action to prevent bigots from expressing their opinions in a way that abuses or offends their co-workers."[3]

With a fine sense of reality, courts have not taken chanting "cunt" at a working woman as conveying the idea "you have a vagina," or as expressing eroticism,[4] but rather as pure abuse.[5] When told such profanity was a simple expletive, one judge was not fooled. If you stubbed your toe, he asked, would you yell, "oh, cunt"?[6] For cultures in which the answer is affirmative, one might ask why women's genitals are a negative expletive. In a similar spirit, neither a shipyard dartboard with a drawing of a woman's breast with a nipple as the bull's eye, nor items like a construction site urinal with a woman's vulva painted on it,[7] has been considered art. A drawing of a nude segmented female torso with "USDA

Choice" stamped on it has not been defended as political satire. The workplace comment "Black women taste like sardines" has not been construed as a possible advertisement for fish, hence protected commercial speech. "It doesn't hurt women to have sex right after childbirth," in the same workplace, has not been seen as an idea of scientific value, however misguided. Graffiti stating, "The more you lick it, the harder it gets" has not been construed as sex education, nor "do you spit or swallow?" as a query expressing concern for oral hygiene.[8]

One Black woman, the only one working in a particular soap factory, reported that soap carved in the shape of a penis was periodically sent down her assembly line.[9] In one restaurant, male management shaped hamburger meat in the form of a penis and asked a woman worker, "Is this big enough?"[10] Another woman who worked in a warehouse charged that male co-workers would expose their buttocks to her.[11] When considering legal action against this type of activity, no one has argued that the soap or hamburger may be artistic expression, the flashing symbolic speech or guerrilla theater, or a male equivalent to nude dancing. When a man slips a woman's paycheck into his pants and requires her to "go for it,"[12] nobody suggests he is making a militant display of dissent against the economic system.

Construing these events as "speech"—in terms of their form as expression and their content as ideas—apparently looks like what it is: a transparent ploy to continue the bigoted abuse and avoid liability. The misogynist meaning and exclusionary impact of such expression have not been contested by most defendants, either. The harm done by this behavior is importantly contextual, certainly, but it is implicitly recognized that social life occurs only in social context, and this is a social harm. That these experiences differ for harasser and harassed is not denied either; this difference seems only to support the fact of their unequal positions in a single shared system of social meaning, further supporting the act as one of inequality. One court rejected the defendant's argument that because racial slurs were common parlance, they did not have racial overtones.[13] Many have rejected defenses that the abuse being litigated was only a joke.[14] The postmodern pose of creative misinterpretation—acting as though words do not mean what they mean or do what they do—has seldom been tried, and even then not to protect the abuse as speech.

In the case of Mechelle Vinson, a Black woman who was sexually abused verbally and raped for two and a half years by her Black male bank supervisor, the U.S. Supreme Court held for the first time that employees have "the right to work in an environment free from discriminatory intimidation, ridicule, and insult."[15] The decision did not separate the verbal from the physical environment, saying control the behavior but protect the speech. Far less did the Court attempt to separate what the rape expressed from what it did. It did not call Mechelle Vinson "offended" and tell her to take it like a man. The Court's formulation of the injury not only relied on knowing what the verbal acts meant as inseparable from the injury they did; it focused the concept of harm—intimidation, ridicule, insult—on what the words particularly did through the meaning they conveyed. These are harms of communication as such. The vocabulary of rape speaks volumes, no doubt saying what it says in the most effective possible way, and with cross-cultural intelligibility. Yet neither the rapes nor the perpetrator's words were considered protected speech because they conveyed meaning or required "mental intermediation"—like knowing the language—to do their damage. The harm of a hostile environment was recognized as a harm of sexual abuse.

The point is, for fifteen years courts have shown real comprehension that what might be called speech, if forced into an abstract First Amendment mold, are in fact acts of inequality, hence actionable as discrimination. Although sexual harassment might be characterized as "sexual expression,"[16] it has never been suggested that its regulation must meet obscenity standards. Actions against racial harassment at work have not been held to constitutional standards for group defamation or incitement either. Under discrimination laws, courts have taken legal action against group-based invective, no matter that it contains ideas or seeks to express or further a political position.[17] Indeed, its role in furthering the politics—that is, the reality—of inequality has been understood as integral to its injuriousness. "KKK" on workplace walls[18] has not been protected as political advocacy, and whether or not violence is imminently incited by it has not mattered. The term "nigger-rigged" has not been protected as merely offensive or satire or hyperbole.[19] A noose hanging over an African-American's work station[20] has not been construed as symbolic speech or protected as discussion of a disfavored subject. Scrawled notes of "African monkeys, why don't you go back to the jungle?"[21] have not been regarded as nonlibelous proposals for a nice tropical vacation.

Beyond simply not being regarded as a problem, the very same terms of group threat and denigration that form the basis of sexual and racial harassment suits have also routinely provided the required evidence of the mental state called "discriminatory intent" for suits against other forms of discrimination.[22] The fact that such verbal behavior serves as a vehicle for a bigoted ideology has not made it protected expression; it has identified the behavior, and other acts surrounding it, as discrimination. Under discrimination law, such expression is not a political opinion; it is a smoking gun. This mental element makes events into discrimination which might otherwise be regarded as coincidence or accident. In other words, *because of* their mental location and content, these words are not only potentially discriminatory in themselves; they are part of the proof that other acts are discriminatory.[23]

The area of sexual and racial harassment has not been without traces of speechlike thinking. One court held that women workers must tolerate pornography posted at work because they are surrounded by it everywhere else.[24] Another said, in reference to the general level of discourse at this workplace, "we must discount the impact of [specific] obscenities in an atmosphere otherwise pervaded by obscenity."[25] A comparable case on racist verbal and visual attacks held, to the contrary, that prejudicial language may be socially pervasive in society, but Congress has decided that discrimination in employment will not be tolerated.[26] Most courts have refused to set the standards for equality law by the standards of abuse set by an unequal society.[27]

Some commentators have suggested that harassment should be illegal only when it is "directed at" an individual.[28] This is the same line that implicitly divides group from individual libel, such that, for First Amendment purposes, individual libel can be regulated but group libel cannot be. The idea seems to be that injury to one person is legally actionable, but the same injury to thousands of people is protected speech. This approach is in tension with the concept of the injury of discrimination as such, in which an individual is hurt only *as* a member of a group.[29] Courts have generally understood, without needing to say so, that group-based attacks are directed at every individual group member within range. Does any Black man doubt, upon encountering "Nigger Die" at work, that it means him? Are graffiti against Black women "directed at" only Black women, pornography using blonde women only at blondes, lesbian epithets only at women who are lesbians? Or is it "directed at" you only if your individual name is on it? Is using a photograph of Martin Luther King, Jr. for target practice at a firing range only "directed at" Dr. King?[30] What target group can afford to find out?

In general, racial and sexual harassment have been the discriminatory acts in court that they are in life until recently, when two contested areas escalated and converged. Women complained that pornography at work constituted sexual harassment in employment, and universities prohibited racial harassment on campus on the model of existing sexual harassment prohibitions. Suddenly, harassment became an issue of speech. Practices of bigotry and inequality were transformed into discussions and debates. Threats became statements of political ideology. What had been judicially understood as acts of discrimination became a dialogue about ideas.

In a case involving pornography as sexual harassment, the employer argued that pornography at work was protected expression, something the workers at Jacksonville Shipyards wanted to *say* to first-class welder Lois Robinson, their opinions about women and sex. Their "views" included naked women supposedly having sex with each other; a woman masturbating herself with a towel; a nude woman on a heater control box with fluid coming from her vaginal area; a woman with long blonde hair (like Lois) wearing only high heels and holding a whip (one welding tool is called a "whip"); and countless women in full labial display. When Lois Robinson protested, the men engaged in more of what the ACLU brief against her termed "speech" by posting a sign stating "Men Only."[31] Suddenly, because Lois Robinson's sexual harassment complaint centered on pornography, her sexual harassment claim invoked the First Amendment, at least so far as relief was concerned.

In the same period, "Death Nigger" was found scratched on a woman's door at Purdue. Elsewhere, "A mind is a terrible thing to waste—especially on a nigger" was left on a blackboard. Still elsewhere a fraternity elected a "Jewish American Princess." Another fraternity held a "slave auction" at which white pledges in blackface performed skits parroting Black entertainers. "Death to all Arabs!! Die Islamic scumbags!" was found scrawled on a university wall.[32] At still another school, a gay student was denounced as a "faggot" and told he did not belong at the university.[33] Swastikas are flown. Crosses are burned. Holocaust revisionism is openly taught in some places.[34] Suddenly all this, too, is said to be a potential constitutional right.

A previously submerged tension is emerging between equality rights as they have long been recognized, in which discriminatory expression is without question a discriminatory act, and a current direction in First Amendment interpretation. This tension is not resolved by the observation, however true it is, that the workplace and the university have always been subject to different rules.[35] Speech has always been more restricted at work and more protected at school, but equality has been equally firmly mandated in both. The fact is, the workplace and the academy are the sites of this confrontation not only because inequality is crucially enacted there, but because equality is crucially guaranteed there. Equality is not generally legally guaranteed in social life. Discriminatory expression does deprive targeted groups of equality elsewhere; no recognized right to equality exists to assert against that deprivation elsewhere. Criminal laws against group defamation have been the closest approximation, but they have seldom been enforced, and they have never been equality laws.

Most courts that have looked at pornography as sexual harassment at work have prohibited it as sex discrimination. None has protected it as speech.[36] But university policies prohibiting harassment on campus have been denounced in and out of court as intolerable restrictions on academic inquiry and violations of freedom of speech.[37] Educational equality, the schools' interest in the regulations at issue, is barely mentioned. What had been bigoted acts and terrorist threats suddenly become conversational gambits, theoretical trial balloons, and incipient poetry. The clear workplace precedents recognizing sexual harassment as sex discrimination are considered barely, if at all.

Most university policies and procedures treat sexual and racial harassment as indistinguishable, while the courts that have invalidated all or part of these codes have treated them as having little in common. Universities often miss that harassment policies raise a variety of expressive issues, while courts miss their common equality foundations and goals. One result is that attempts to defend regulation of racial harassment in education on the basis of sexual precedents have not been persuasive, yet decisions invalidating racial harassment codes threaten to take sexual harassment regulations down with them. An explicit sex-to-race analogy has not worked to support the codes, but an implicit race-to-sex analogy is being used to undermine them.

Racial and sexual harassment, separately and together, promote inequality, violate oppressed groups, work to destroy their social standing and repute, and target them for discrimination from contempt to genocide. Yet each also has a particular history, occupies its own ground, and works in its own way, both as expression and as inequality. Racial and sexual harassment function just as actively, separately and together, in social inequality; both need to be stopped. They are no different in the severity of impact on victims or in the degree of damage they inflict on equality rights. They differ primarily in the mechanism through which they work on perpetrators. Because of this, they relate differently to the reality of the inequality in which they arise and intervene and raise some distinct expressive concerns.

For expressive purposes, the distinction that matters, in my view, is not between harassment based on race and harassment based on gender, which are often inseparable in any case, but between speech that is sex and speech that is not. Harassment that is sexual is a sex act, like pornography. Harassment that is not sexual works more through its content, as the traditional model of group defamation envisions, however hateful and irrational, however viscerally it plays on prejudice, however damaging to equality rights.

By harassment that is not explicitly sexual,[38] I mean teachers' saying that women students are no good at this subject or calling on only men, or scholarship purporting to document the superiority of some racial groups over others, or statements in a workplace like, "There's nothing worse than having to work around women."[39] It is amazing how few examples there are in this category, and how much of what might be simply gender or racial harassment proves on deeper examination to be sexual, like "Women are only fit company for something that howls."[40]

Sexuality is a central dynamic in gender; sexuality and gender converge in the world. Consider the man who placed an explicitly sexual picture on the desk of a woman co-worker "with a note saying something like, 'You should be doing this instead of a man's job.'"[41] All sexual harassment, including that against women and men of color specifically, is gendered. A great deal of harassment that is sexual is expressly racist. Examples include: "Jew faggot,"[42] "Black bitches suck cock,"[43] "Niggers are a living example that the Indians screwed buffalo,"[44] and the endless references to the penis size of African-American men.[45] Laws against defamation often prohibit publications that "portray . . . unchastity . . . of a class of citizens, of any race, color, creed, or religion . . ."[46] specifically. This refers to the men as well as the women in these groups. The fact that these laws have never been applied to racist pornography, in which women of color are routinely presented as "unchaste," suggests that portrayal of "unchastity" in women is regarded as just life, or perhaps that only unchastity in men is a racial insult. But it has not been applied to the pornography using men of color either.

Sexual words and pictures, delivered in context, work the way pornography works: they do not merely describe sexuality or represent it. In a sense, they have sex. When a man sends a note ending, "I'm going to fuck you even if I have to *rape* you,"[47] he is getting off on writing and sending the note and envisioning the recipient reading it. The recipient feels sexually violated as well as terrified of rape. (Need I add, this has nothing to do with the use of the term "fuck" as such.)[48] When male workers say, "Hey pussycat, come here and give me a whiff,"[49] it is a sexual invasion, an act of sexual aggression, a violation of sexual boundaries, a sex act in itself.

I am not ultimately sure why this is the case, but it has something to do with the positioning of sex words in sexual abuse, in abuse as sex, in sex as abuse, in sex. Words of sexual abuse are integral to acts of sexual abuse from birth to after death. As incantations while sexual abuse is occurring, they carry that world with them, such that to utter them is to let loose in the body the feeling of doing it, and sex is done largely for the purpose of creating that feeling. The more pornography invades the sexuality of a population, the more widespread this dynamic becomes. It is not so much that the sexual terms reference a reality as that they reaccess and restimulate body memory of it for both aggressor and victim. The aggressor gets an erection; the victim screams and struggles and bleeds and blisters and becomes five years old. "Being offended" is the closest the First Amendment tradition comes to grasping this effect.

This process of empowerment of the perpetrator and traumatization of the victim occurs not because of the content of the words in the usual sense but because of the experiences they embody and convey. For this function of words carrying lived reality from one place to another, it matters that the physical tortures that accompany the words are being inflicted on a mass scale on women as a group. It matters that children are being sexually abused as the words of abuse are spoken and pictures taken. It matters that electrodes are being applied to the genitals of women being called "cunt" in photography studios in Los Angeles and the results mass-marketed. In Argentina under the junta, when people were rounded up and tortured and disappeared because they were Jewish, "Jew" used as a taunt and term of torture had such a meaning.[50]

This is only to say the obvious: just as language shapes social reality, the social reality of language in use determines what it conveys and means and does, such that to say that these words do not have this meaning or do these things is to say that this social reality does not exist. Were there no such thing as male supremacy, and were it not sexualized, there would be no such injury as sexual harassment. Words do not do it alone, of course, but what sexual harassment does, only words can do— or, rather, the harm of sexual harassment can be done only through expressive means.

The social coding of sexuality as intimate and pleasurable also contributes to the distinctive sting and intrusiveness of harassment that is sexual. Sexuality is defined as intimacy as such; nothing else goes onto you or into you in the same way. One is socially called to participate in sexuality with one's most intimate self. Sexual abuse is further unique in that the victim is expected to enjoy it. Perpetrators of racial abuse experience pleasure that may be said to be sexual in the sense of the thrill of dominance, whether or not it becomes literally orgasmic; the victims are not expected to enjoy it. Sex as a form of abuse demands and exacts pleasure from the victim as well, both fake and at times tragically real. It probably still needs to be said that this does not mean that the victims want the abuse. The forced complicity of the manipulated response of the victim's body is part of the injury and attaches both to the abusive relation and to the words that go with it.

Because of its location in intimacy, harassment that is sexual peculiarly leaves nothing between you and it: it begins in your family, your primary connections, those through which the self is developed. Sexual abuse occurs most often within one's own family and community. With harassment that is not sexual, for example religious or ethnic, the target has a family, a community reviled together, an "us" that defies being defined by this treatment by "them." Someone is on your side, someone to go home to, rather than to run away from home from. This does not keep the shame from burning, the self-revulsion from attacking your body, or the despair from cannibalizing your future, just as with sexual abuse. It does provide a separation that says this is not just you, this is not all there is to you.

For at least these reasons, speech that is sex has a different relation to reality than speech that is not sex has. Sexual harassment, because it is sexual, and because of the place of words and images in sex, and the place of sex in life, manipulates the perpetrator's socialized body relatively primitively and directly, as pornography does, and often because pornography already has. This is men's beloved "hard-wiring," giving them that exculpatory sense that the sexual desires so programmed are natural and so operate before and beyond their minds— got there before they did, as it were. But it is nothing more than social conditioning. Put another way, if First Amendment protected thought is what men are doing while masturbating to pornography, raping employees while saying, "Just like I could hire you, I could fire you,"[51] and shouting "cunt" in a crowded shipyard, every mental blip short of a flat EEG is First Amendment protected speech. Whatever mental process is imagined to be involved in consuming pornography, it has not stopped obscenity from being placed beyond First Amendment protection, either.

Moreover, there is no evidence that consumers of racist propaganda aggress against the target of the literature whether or not they agree with the positions it takes.[52] This is not to say that such material works wholly on the conscious level, but rather that it does not primarily work by circumventing conscious processes. The same can be said for nonsexually explicit misogynist literature. With pornography, by contrast, consumers see women as less than human, and even rape them, without being aware that an "idea" promoting that content, far less a political position in favor of the sexualized inequality of the sexes, is being advanced. Rape myth acceptance scale scores soar without conscious awareness that attitudes on women and rape are being manipulated through manipulating sexual responses. Nothing analogous to the sexual response has been located as the mechanism of racism, or as the mechanism of response to sexist material that is not sexual.

One way to think about issues of expressive freedom here is to ask whether something works through thought or not through thought. An argument that some races or genders or sexual persuasions are inferior to others is an argument—an antiegalitarian argument, a false argument, a pernicious argument, an argument for hate and for hierarchy, but an argument nonetheless. It is an act of inequality of a particular kind, whose consequences for social inequality need to be confronted on constitutional terrain where equality and speech converge, in a context as sensitive to the need for equality guarantees in the law of speech as for speech guarantees in the law of equality. So-called speech that works as a sex act is not an argument. An orgasm is not an argument and cannot be argued with. Compared with a thought, it raises far less difficult speech issues, if it raises any at all.

Considering the dynamics of racism is complicated by the difficulty of knowing what drives it. Given all the damage it has done, and its persistence and adaptability across time and space, there can be no doubt that it is deep and strong and explosive. Perhaps sexuality is a dynamic in racism and ethnic prejudice as well as in gender bias. Upon examination, much racist behavior is sexual. Consider the pure enjoyment of dominance that makes power its own reward, reports of the look of pleasure on the face of racist torturers, accounts of the adrenalin high of hatred and excitement that survivors of lynchings describe having seen, the sexual atrocities always involved. Recall the elaborate use of race, ethnicity, and religion for sexual excitement in pornography and in much racist harassment. Remember the racially coded sex and marriage taboos and titillations and targetings in white supremacist societies, the sexual denigration pervasive in anti-Semitism. Once the benefits and functions of much racial murder, torture, hatred, and dominance, perhaps even economic supremacy, are exposed as sexual, its rationalizations as natural, converging with gender on the ideological level, what of racism is left to explain? Something, but what?

So far I have been discussing words of abuse uttered by dominant others and the way they work as acts of inequality. That sexual words make sex happen, with extended effects on women, is further supported by observing what happens when victims of sexual harassment speak the abuser's words, testifying to what he said. When she says what he said, what is she *doing*? Anita Hill's allegations of sexual harassment by Clarence Thomas in his confirmation hearing for the Supreme Court show how sexual words work as acts in racism and sexism by showing what happens when a woman, a Black woman, speaks in public the sex words a man spoke, in isolation, to her.

In this episode, the language of sexual abuse collided with the language of public discourse; women's reality collided with everyday politics as usual, the distance between the two measured by one word: credibility. When speech is sex, it determines what is taken as real. The more the abuse sounds like the coverup language of public speech, the less it sounds like what he really said, the more credible she is. By this standard, Professor Hill's earlier accounts were the most credible: "he spoke about acts that he had seen in pornographic films." Less credible were "Long Dong Silver" and "who put pubic hair on my Coke?" The speakable words were "[he] told me graphically of his own sexual prowess." We then heard the long breath of the woman passing the point of no return in what can now be done to her preceding, "He also spoke on some occasions of the pleasures he had given to women," then the pause, the drop in her voice, before speaking even the clinical words "with oral sex."[53]

We heard the spoken voice of a woman uttering the sounds of abuse, the moment in which silence breaks on the unspeakability of the experience, the echo of what had been unheard. Much of the response was disbelief, the reaffirmation of the silence of "nothing happened," the attempt to push the uncomfortable reality back underground through pathologizing dismissal. This was done through big words like "mendacity," little words like "lie," and halfway-in-between words like "fantasy." In Patricia Williams' incisive analysis, Anita Hill was said to be "consciously lying but fantasizing truth."[54]

What happens when you put the real language of sexual abuse in a Senate confirmation hearing? It is a lot like putting a videotape of your rape in your rape trial. It, and you, are treated as if you do not belong, as if you pulled down your pants and defecated in public. You are lowered by proving your injury. He is not. He allegedly said these things. If they were said, they were *his* words. She said them in quotation marks. But it is the woman to whom they are attributed when she speaks them. When she says them, it is believed they are true *of her* somehow, but not believed of him. Senator Grassley called it "an offensive story." Deborah Norville, a radio commentator, "left feeling dirty somehow." President Bush "felt unclean watching it."[55] The offensiveness, the dirt, the uncleanness stick to the woman, the woman of color in particular.

Women know this. It explains their fear of speaking about sexual abuse in public, their sense of reviolation when doing so, their shame. It is because of how they are seen. It explains why an account like Anita Hill's developed, with a consistent perpetrator sexuality, from the telescoped expressions of unhappiness to her friends at the time to the minimal FBI sketch to the fuller details when pushed on cross-examination before the Senate committee. As she put it, she told it to her level of comfort. I felt she did not want his words in her mouth. Women do not want to be pornography. When words of sexual abuse are in our mouths, that is pornography, and we become pornography because that is what pornography is.

Once you are used for sex, you are sexualized. You lose your human status. You are sex, therefore unworthy of belief and impossible to violate. Your testimony that you were sexually abused proves your abuse, which defines you as sex, which makes it incredible and impossible that you were sexually abused. In a world made by pornography, testimony about sexual harassment is live oral pornography starring the victim. Because the account becomes a form of sex, the abuse is rendered consensual in the mind of the viewer.

There is nothing else like this: because she *says* she was hurt, it is believed she had a wonderful time. Because she *says* what happened, it is believed that it could not have happened to *her*. Only words; but because they are sex, the speaker as well as the spoken-about is transformed into sex. This is a dynamic common to sexual harassment and pornography. When talking sex is having sex, as talking pornography was sexual harassment in this case, exposing the reality of sexual harassment can become a kind of pornography, and exposing the reality of pornography, as lived, can become a kind of harassment.

In the Thomas-Hill hearings, and in the social upheaval surrounding them, race and gender were discussed, revealing many questionable social attitudes. But sex, with all its racial dimensions, was what was done. What was done to Anita Hill, both in Clarence Thomas' office ten years before, and to a lesser extent in the Senate chamber when she testified to it, was sex *happening*. It was not simply sex being *discussed*. Talking about sex can be speech, but doing it through words can be sexual assault. Harassment that is not sexual does its harm through its content, undermining equality, especially in universities, where the mind is the terrain of the equality as well as the speech. Harassment that is sexual does its harm as an act of sexual abuse, like, and sometimes as, pornography.

The law of sexual harassment has found no way to challenge women's lack of sexual credibility, the presumption that women fantasize or ask for sexual abuse, a presumption considered proved when we recount the abuse itself. Neither has the law of rape, in spite of its attempts to keep women's sexual history out of rape trials and dignify women's testimony. The challenge to pornography as sex inequality is the first time this dynamic has been confronted directly, by any law existing or proposed. Now resistance to that challenge, through invoking speech protection for pornography at work, is being used to attempt to undermine existing protections from sexual harassment and racial harassment as well. Stopping pornography, and with it the sexualization of aggression and legitimized use of women from brothels to courtrooms, is women's only chance to gain, in or out of court, a voice that cannot be used against us.

III

▼

EQUALITY

AND

SPEECH

▼

THE LAW OF EQUALITY and the law of freedom of speech are on a collision course in this country. Until this moment, the constitutional doctrine of free speech has developed without taking equality seriously—either the problem of social inequality or the mandate of substantive legal equality. Originally, of course, the Constitution contained no equality guarantee to serve as context, expansion joint, handmaiden, counterbalance, or coequal goal to the speech guarantee. Yet the modern doctrine of speech dates from considerably after the entrenchment of equality in the Fourteenth Amendment,[1] and still the First Amendment has been interpreted, with a few exceptions, as if it were not there.

More precisely, the First Amendment has grown as if a commitment to speech were no part of a commitment to equality and as if a commitment to equality had no implications for the law of speech—as if the upheaval that produced the Reconstruction Amendments did not move the ground under the expressive freedom, setting new limits and mandating new extensions, perhaps even demanding reconstruction of the speech right itself. The version of equality that *has* become part of First Amendment law has been negative—equally keeping law from regulating one forum or view as another—and formal—speech protected for one group or interest is equally protected for others.[2] It is, in other words, largely redundant. The subprovince of the First Amendment that resonates in equal protection is simply an unbiased extension of precedent and the rule of law—a narrow equality supporting a shallow speech. Fourteenth Amendment equality, for its part, has grown as if equality could be achieved while the First Amendment protected the speech of inequality, meaning whenever inequality takes an expressive form, and without considering equal access to speech as central to any equality agenda.

Both bodies of law accordingly show virtually total insensitivity to the damage done to social equality by expressive means and a substantial lack of recognition that some people get a lot more speech than others.[3] In the absence of these recognitions, the power of those who have speech has become more and more exclusive, coercive, and violent as it has become more and more legally protected. Understanding that there is a relationship between these two issues—the less speech you have, the more the speech of those who have it keeps you unequal; the more the speech of the dominant is protected, the more dominant they become and the less the subordinated are heard from—is virtually nonexistent. Issues at the equality-speech interface are not framed as problems of balance between two cherished constitutional goals, or as problems of meaningful access to either right in the absence of the other, but as whether the right to free speech is infringed acceptably or unacceptably. Equality-promoting provisions on hate crimes, campus harassment, and pornography,[4] for example, tend to be attacked and defended solely in terms of the damage they do, or do not do, to speech. At the same time, issues such as racial segregation in education, with its accompanying illiteracy and silence, are framed solely in equality terms, rather than also as official barriers to speech and therefore as violations of the First Amendment.[5]

First Amendment speech and Fourteenth Amendment equality have never contended on constitutional terrain. The reason is largely that both have been interpreted more negatively than positively, prohibiting violations by government more than chartering legal intervention for social change, even as governmental inaction and the more extended consequences of governmental action undermine this distinction in both areas. It is also relevant that federal equality statutes have not been seen to arise under the Fourteenth Amendment, although it expressly authorizes them,[6] and action by states against social inequalities needs no constitutional authority, so invokes the Constitution only when said to violate it.

This mutual one-sidedness in the law has made it virtually impossible to create a community of comprehension that there is a relation, for example, between the use of the epithet "nigger" and the fact that a disproportionate number of children who go to bed hungry every night in this country are African-American; or the use of the word "cunt" and the fact that most prostitutes are women. It creates no room to see that slave codes that made it a crime to teach a slave to read, or schools in which Black children cannot learn to write, deny them freedom of speech; or that judicially eliminating grievance procedures that recognize racist or homophobic vilification as barriers to education officially denies students equality in education.[7] The tensions and intersections between the deeper principles and wider orbits of equality and speech remain unmapped, equality unspeaking and speech unequal.

The official history of speech in the United States is not a history of inequality—unlike in Europe, where the role of hate propaganda in the Holocaust has not been forgotten. In America, the examples that provide the life resonance of the expressive freedom, the backdrop of atrocities for the ringing declarations, derive mostly from attempts to restrict the political speech of communists during the McCarthy era. Through this trauma, the country relearned its founding lesson: not to stifle political dissent. Horrible consequences to careers, families, privacy, and security resulted from attempts that now look paranoid to shut up what mostly good and creative people could think and say, from academic theory to street advocacy, about the form of government and economic system we should have. The story of the First Amendment is an epic story of overcoming that, of progress, of making sure it never happens again.

The litany predicated on this experience goes like this. The evil to be avoided is government restricting ideas because it disagrees with the content of their political point of view. The terrain of struggle is the mind; the dynamic at work is intellectual persuasion; the risk is that marginal, powerless, and relatively voiceless dissenters, with ideas we will never hear, will be crushed by governmental power. This has become the "speech you hate" test: the more you disagree with content, the more important it becomes to protect it. You can tell you are being principled by the degree to which you abhor what you allow. The worse the speech protected, the more principled the result. There is a faith that truth will prevail if left alone, often expressed in an openly competitive laissez-faire model taken from bourgeois economics and applied to the expressive marketplace: the "marketplace of ideas" metaphor.[8] The marketplace becomes the battlefield when we are assured that truth will prevail while grappling in open encounter with falsehood, to paraphrase Milton, as he so often is.[9]

In this faith, restricting some speech can only eventuate in restricting more or all speech: the "slippery slope" hazard.[10] Restricting speech is seen to be tempting, to have a seductive power that draws governments to its totalitarian—also regarded as principled—logic: if we restrict this bad thing now, we will not be able to stop ourselves from restricting this good thing later. One corollary is that everyone has an interest in everyone else's speech being free, because restriction will get around to you eventually; the less power you have, the sooner it will get around to you. Crucial is that speech cannot be restricted because you fear its consequences: the "bad tendency" or "witch-hunt" doctrine. If some speech is conceded to be risky, more speech to the contrary will eliminate that risk. Most of all, government can make no judgment as to content.[11] For constitutional purposes, there is no such thing as a false idea,[12] there are only more or less "offensive" ones,[13] to remedy which, love of liberty recommends averting the eyes[14] or growing a thicker skin.

Americans are taught this view by about the fourth grade[15] and continue to absorb it through osmosis from everything around them for the rest of their lives, including law school, to the point that those who embrace it think it is their own personal faith, their own original view, and trot it out like something learned from their own personal lives every time a problem is denominated one of "speech," whether it really fits or not. Any issue that strikes this chord, however faintly, gets played this tune, even if the consequences are more like a replay of McCarthyism than resistance to it. This approach is adhered to with a fundamentalist zeal even when it serves to protect lies, silence dissent, destroy careers, intrude on associations, and retard change. At least as ironic is the fact that the substance of the left's forbidden theories, which were a kind of argument for class equality, made no impression on the law of speech at all.

Has this doctrinal edifice guaranteed free and equal speech? These days, censorship occurs less through explicit state policy than through official and unofficial privileging of powerful groups and viewpoints. This is accomplished through silencing in many forms and enforced by the refusal of publishers and editors to publish, or publish well, uncompromised expressions of dissent that make them uncomfortable by challenging the distribution of power, including sexual power. Such publishing decisions, no matter how one-sided and cumulative and exclusionary, are regarded as the way the system of freedom of expression is supposed to work. Legal accountability for these decisions is regarded as fascism; social accountability for them is regarded as creeping fascism; the decisions themselves are regarded as freedom of speech. Speech theory does not disclose or even consider how to deal with power vanquishing powerlessness; it tends to transmute this into truth vanquishing falsehood, meaning what power wins becomes considered true. Speech, hence the lines within which much of life can be lived, belongs to those who own it, mainly big corporations.

Refusals to publish works that criticize the sexual distribution of power in particular are often, in my experience, supported by reference to the law of libel. Libel law, just one subdivision of the law of speech which lacks sensitivity to the substance of social inequality, has become a tool for justifying refusals to publish attacks on those with power, even as it targets the powerless for liability. Its equality-blindness goes back at least to the formative *New York Times v. Sullivan*,[16] in which the law of libel was first recognized as coming under the First Amendment. The *New York Times* ran a civil rights fundraising ad for Black leaders that described racist misbehavior by white police in the South. On the basis of minor inaccuracies in the ad, the *Times* was successfully sued for libel under state law by the police commissioner of Montgomery, Alabama. The newspaper argued that more than minor inaccuracies should be required to sue for a form of speech. When the *Times* won this argument before the Supreme Court, a new First Amendment doctrine was born.

In reality, *Sullivan* was animated by issues of substantive equality as powerful as they were submerged; indeed, they were perceptible only in the facts. The case lined up an equality interest—that of the civil rights activists in the content of the ad—*with* the First Amendment interest of the newspaper. This aligned sentiment in favor of racial equality with holding libel law to standards of speech protection higher than state law would likely enforce on racists. In other words, *Sullivan* used support for civil rights to make it easier for newspapers to publish defamatory falsehoods without being sued.[17] This brigading of support for racial equality with enhanced power for the media to be less careful about what they publish was utterly tacit. The argument for the *Times* by Herbert Wechsler—originator of the broadside attack on *Brown v. Board of Education,* which prohibited racial segregation in the public schools, as unprincipled constitutional adjudication—did not mention equality at all, while benefitting from the pro-equality wind at its back.[18]

Because the *Times* won without any acknowledgment that concern for substantive equality powered this extension of the First Amendment, the decision did not consider whether the standard of care for truth might have been drawn higher if, for example, southern racist police had been accused of libeling prominent leaders of the nascent civil rights movement in an ad with a few inaccuracies. The extent to which publishers had to know the truth before they could recklessly disregard it, as *Sullivan* newly required for libel of public figures, might have appeared especially problematic if the submerged equality issues had been exposed. Bigotry as often produces unconscious lies as knowing ones, indeed often precludes the dominant from seeing the truth of inequality being lived out beneath their station, hence vision. The implications for subordinated groups of a relaxed standard of truth for publishers—perhaps the stake of the subordinated in having publishers substantiate what they print might be as often on the other side? perhaps media are owned and run by dominant groups who sincerely see a dominant way of seeing as the truth?—was not discussed. Nor was social inequality considered when, in the same case, the constitutional status of laws against group defamation was undermined in advance of a real case on the subject.[19]

The resulting law of libel has had the effect of licensing the dominant to say virtually anything about subordinated groups with impunity while supporting the media's power to refuse access to speech to the powerless, as it can always cite fear of a libel suit by an offended powerful individual. This situation is exacerbated by the facts that it is subordinated groups who are damaged by group defamation and mostly the privileged who can make credible threats to sue even for true statements that make them look bad. Because the *Sullivan* holding made it easier for media to get away with false and damaging statements about public figures, individuals from subordinated groups who take on dominant interests in public are left especially exposed—sexually libeled feminists who oppose pornography, for example.[20] The assumption seems to be that anyone who stands up in public has the same power that government and its officials do, and possesses access to speech equal to that of socially privileged or unscrupulous operatives of the status quo, like pornographers.

The *Sullivan* dictum on group libel substantially undermined the vitality of an earlier case, *Beauharnais v. Illinois*,[21] which had held that group defamation, including publications that expose the citizens of any race, color, creed, or religion to contempt, could be made criminal, without violating the First Amendment. *Sullivan* tilted First Amendment law in the direction of the conclusion that individual libel is actionable but group libel is not, making injury to the reputation of individuals legally real and consigning injury to the reputation of groups to legal limbo. Reputational harm to those who are allowed to be individuals—mostly white men—is legal harm. Those who are defined by, and most often

falsely maligned through, their membership in groups—
namely almost everyone else—have no legal claim. Indeed, those who harm them have something of a speech
right to do that harm. This arrangement avoids the
rather obvious reality that groups are made up of individuals. It also looks a lot like discrimination against
harms done through discrimination, in favor of what are
regarded by distinction as individual harms. In reality,
libel of groups multiplies rather than avoids the very
same damage through reputation which the law of individual libel recognizes when done one at a time, as well
as inflicting some of its own.

The effectiveness of *Sullivan*'s undermining of
Beauharnais became vividly clear in the later case that
arose out of the Nazis' proposed march in Skokie, Illinois, a site chosen because it was largely populated by
Jewish survivors of the Holocaust. The march was found
to be protected speech, invalidating a group defamation
law that would have stopped it, by judges who had never
faced a pogrom piously intoning how much they ab-
horred what the Nazis had to say, but how legally their
hands were tied and how principled they were in allowing it. You can tell how principled they were because of
how much they hated the speech.

Over a notable dissent by Justice Blackmun, the U.S.
Supreme Court denied review,[22] leaving this result
standing and leaving unvindicated a perception on fas-

cist speech by Justice Jackson in a dissent of a decade before: "These terse epithets come down to our generation weighted with hatreds accumulated through centuries of bloodshed. They are recognized words of art in the profession of defamation... They are always, and in every context, insults which do not spring from reason and can be answered by none. Their historical associations with violence are well understood, both by those who hurl and those who are struck by these missiles."[23] Justice Jackson was later to dissent in *Beauharnais,* but when he wrote this, he had just returned from the Nuremberg trials, facing what those who became the residents of Skokie had survived.

Nobody mentioned that to be liquidated because of one's group membership is the ultimate inequality. Constitutional equality has never been the interest that hate speech prohibitions are seen to promote.[24] No one to my knowledge has proposed that Congress prohibit hate propaganda to effectuate the Fourteenth Amendment. Instead, when hate speech regulations are assessed, the question has been: does a given law trench too far, or not too far, on the right of free speech? The political speech litany is invoked: nasty ideas that may or may not cause harm, depending on whether they are acted upon (we are supposed to wait); truth outing; more speech solving the problem; swallowing your gorge and adjusting your dignitary standards if you want to be part of the big bad real world. This, under a document that accepts balancing among constitutional interests as method.

The closest the Court has come to recognizing substantive equality in the hate speech area occurred in *Beauharnais*. Writing for the majority, Justice Frankfurter said: "[A] man's job and his educational opportunities and the dignity accorded him may depend as much on the reputation of the racial and religious group to which he willy-nilly belongs, as on his own merits."[25] Employment, education, and human dignity are all on equality territory but went unmarked as such. Civil unrest—otherwise known as oppressed people agitating for their equality or expressing frustration at their inequality—was also noted as a possible consequence of allowing group defamation to go unchecked.

Justice Douglas, in his dissent in *Beauharnais*, came almost as close: "Hitler and his Nazis showed how evil a conspiracy could be which was aimed at destroying a race by exposing it to contempt, derision, and obloquy. I would be willing to concede that such conduct directed at a race or group in this country could be made an indictable offense. For such a project would be more than the exercise of free speech."[26] He does not say what that more would be an exercise in. Kalven writes of this passage, "There is a germ of a powerful idea here," but he does not call that idea by its name either.[27] The statute in *Beauharnais* was not defended as an equality law, and no argument in the case located group defamation as part of social inequality.[28] Legal equality under the Fourteenth Amendment, in effect for almost a hundred years, was not mentioned.

So there never has been a fair fight in the United States between equality and speech as two constitutional values, equality supporting a statute or practice, speech challenging it. Courts have balanced *statutory* equality interests against the constitutional speech protection. Equality always won these fights until pornography, statutorily framed as sex inequality, lost to the First Amendment, and now equality is losing to speech-based attacks on hate provisions as well.[29] In other words, pornography ordinances and hate crime provisions fail constitutional scrutiny that they might, with constitutional equality support, survive. Moreover, speech is not extended that might be, as in the broadcasting or campaign financing areas.[30] If speech were seen through an equality lens, nude dancing regulations might be tailored to ending the sex inequality of prostitution, at the same time undermining the social credibility of the pimp's lie that public sex is how women express themselves. Crossburning prohibitions would be seen as the civil rights protections they are. Women might be seen to have a sex equality right to the speech of abortion counseling.[31] Poverty might even be seen as the inequality underlying street begging, at once supporting the speech interest in such solicitations and suggesting that equal access to speech might begin before all one can say is "spare change?"[32]

Since this perspective does not yet animate case law, speech cases that consider words as triggers to violent action instead submerge inequality issues further. In *Brandenburg v. Ohio,* a case that set the standard on speech and consequent conduct with regard to inflammatory advocacy, the words were Ku Klux Klan racism.[33] *Claiborne Hardware,* a further ruling on instigating speech, questioned whether the arm-twisting rhetoric of leaders of a civil rights boycott was protected or whether the activists could be held responsible for the lost business in money damages.[34] *Brandenburg*'s concern was whether the "ideas" of the Klan were a sufficient "incitement" to restrict the speech, meaning were they immediate enough to the assaults. *Claiborne Hardware* explored the parameters of holding public speakers responsible for the consequences of their persuasive advocacy. Suppressed entirely in the piously evenhanded treatment of the Klan and the boycotters— the studied inability to tell the difference between oppressor and oppressed that passes for principled neutrality in this area as well as others—was the fact that the Klan was promoting inequality and the civil rights leaders were resisting it, in a country that is supposedly not constitutionally neutral on the subject.

If this was expectable, the virtual absence of discussion of equality in recent litigation over discrimination policies that prohibit group-based harassment and bigotry on campuses was astounding. Denominated "campus speech codes" by their opponents, these regulations are formally predicated on federal laws that require equal access to an education on the basis of race and sex.[35] In challenges to these regulations under the First Amendment, which have been successful so far, the statutory equality interest is barely mentioned. That these procedures might vindicate a constitutional interest in equality which is as important as, or part of, the speech interest used to demolish them is not considered. What can one say about the failure to take seriously the educational equality these provisions exist to serve?

Nor is equality recognized as legally relevant to the problem of pornography, which is addressed instead under the First Amendment doctrine of obscenity. Obscenity law started with the "deprave and corrupt the morals of consumers" test (*they're* being hurt); moved through the censorship of literature from Joyce through Radclyffe Hall to Henry Miller, making them all bestsellers (*they're* being hurt); winding up with the Supreme Court devising its own obscenity test,[36] which is so effective that, under it, the pornography industry has quadrupled in size (*they're* being hurt?). The ineffectuality of obscenity law is due in some part to exempting materials of literary, political, artistic, or scientific value. Value can be found in anything, depending, I have come to think, not only on one's adherence to postmodernism, but on how much one is being paid. And never underestimate the power of an erection, these days termed "entertainment," to give a thing value.[37] Adding to the unworkability of the obscenity test is the requirement that the state prove "prurient interest": is the average person turned on? The more violent pornography is, the less willing juries and police are to say it is arousing, and more and more pornography is more and more violent, and arousing.

Equally difficult in practice has been the requirement in the obscenity test that community standards be proven violated. The more pornography there is, the more it sets de facto community standards, conforming views of what is acceptable to what is arousing, even as the stimulus to arousal must be more and more violating to work. In other words, inequality is allowed to set community standards for the treatment of women. What is wrong with pornography is that it hurts women and their equality. What is wrong with obscenity law is that this reality has no role in it. This irrelevant and unworkable tool is then placed in the hands of the state, most of whose actors have little interest in stopping this abuse but a substantial interest in avoiding prosecutions they cannot win. The American law of obscenity, as a result, is only words.

The pornography issue, far more than the political speech cases, has provided the setting for the definitive development of the absolutist approach to speech. First Amendment absolutism did not begin in obscenity cases, but it is in explaining why obscenity should be protected speech, and how it cannot be distinguished from art and literature, that much of the work of absolutism has been done, taking as its point of departure and arrival the position that whatever is expressive should be constitutionally protected. In pornography, absolutism found, gained, and consolidated its ground and hit its emotional nerve. It began as a dissenting position of intellectual extremists and ended by reducing the regulation of obscenity to window dressing on violence against women.[38]

Concretely, observe that it was the prospect of losing access to pornography that impelled the social and legal development of absolutism as a bottom line for the First Amendment, as well as occasioned bursts of passionate eloquence on behalf of speech per se: if we can't have this, they seem to say, what can we have? During the same twenty-year period of struggle over obscenity standards, the Court was watching more and more pornography as its mass-marketed forms became more and more intrusive and aggressive. Observing this process from its end point of state protection of pornography, I have come to think that the main principle at work here is that, once pornography becomes pervasive, speech *will* be defined so that men can have their pornography. American obscenity law merely illustrates one adaptation of this principle: some men ineffectually prohibit it while others vaunt it openly as the standard for speech as such.

Consider the picture. The law against pornography was not designed to see harm to women in the first place. It is further weakened as pornography spreads, expanding into new markets (such as video and computers) and more legitimate forums and making abuse of women more and more invisible as abuse, as that abuse becomes more and more visible as sex. So the Court becomes increasingly *unable to tell* what is pornography and what is not, a failing it laments not as a consequence of the saturation of society by pornography, but as a specifically judicial failure, then finally as an impossibility of line-drawing. The stage is thus set for the transformation of pornography into political speech: the excluded and stigmatized "ideas" we love to hate. Obscured is the way this protects what pornography says and ignores what it does, or, alternatively, protects what pornography says as a means of protecting what it does. Thus can a law develop which prohibits restricting a film because it advocates adultery,[39] but does not even notice a film that is made from a rape.[40]

Nothing in the American law of obscenity is designed to perceive the rape, sexual abuse of children, battering, sexual harassment, prostitution, or sexual murder in pornography. This becomes insulting upon encountering obscenity law's search for harm and failure to find any. The law of child pornography, by contrast—based as it is on the assumption that children are harmed by having sex pictures made of them—applies a test developed in areas of speech other than the sexual: if the harm of speech outweighs its value,[41] it can be restricted by properly targeted means. Given the history of the law of pornography of adult women, it is tempting to regard this as a miracle. Child pornography is not considered the speech of a sexually dissident minority, which it is, advocating "ideas" about children and sex, which it does. Perhaps the fact that boys were used in the film in the test case has something to do with it. The ability to see that child pornography is harmful has everything to do with a visceral sense of the inequality in power between children and adults, yet inequality is never mentioned.

Now, in this context of speech and equality concerns, consider again the judicial opinion on the law Andrea Dworkin and I wrote and Indianapolis passed. This law defines the documented harms pornography does as violations of equality rights and makes them actionable as practices of discrimination, of second-class citizenship. This ordinance allows anyone hurt through pornography to prove its role in their abuse, to recover for the deprivation of their civil rights, and to stop it from continuing. Judicially, this was rendered as censorship of ideas.

In *American Booksellers v. Hudnut*, the Court of Appeals for the Seventh Circuit found that this law violated the First Amendment. It began by recognizing that the harm pornography does is real, conceding that the legislative finding of a causal link was judicially adequate: "... we accept the premises of this legislation. Depictions of subordination tend to perpetuate subordination. The subordinate status of women in turn leads to affront and lower pay at work, insult and injury at home, battery and rape on the streets. In the language of the legislature, '[p]ornography is central in creating and maintaining sex as a basis of discrimination.'"[42] Writing for the panel, Judge Easterbrook got, off and on, that "subordination" is something pornography does, not something it just says, and that its active role had to be proven in each case brought under the ordinance. But he kept losing his mental bearings and referring to pornography as an "idea,"[43] finally concluding that the harm it does "demonstrates the power of pornography as speech."[44] This is like saying that the more a libel destroys a reputation, the greater is its power as speech. To say that the more harm speech does, the more protected it is, is legally wrong, even in this country.

Implicitly applying the political speech model, Judge Easterbrook said that the law restricted the marketplace of ideas, the speech of outcast dissenters—referring presumably to those poor heads of organized crime families making ten billion dollars a year trafficking women. He said the law discriminated on the basis of point of view, establishing an approved view of what could be said and thought about women and sex. He failed to note at this point that the invalidated causes of action included coercion, force, and assault, rather a far cry from saying and thinking. He reminded us of *Sullivan,* whose most famous dictum is that to flourish, debate must be "uninhibited, robust, and wide-open."[45] Behind his First Amendment facade, women were being transformed into ideas, sexual traffic in whom was protected as if it were a discussion, the men uninhibited and robust, the women wide-open.

Judge Easterbrook did not say this law was not a sex discrimination law, but he gave the state interest it therefore served—opposition to sex inequality—no constitutional weight. He did this by treating it as if it were a group defamation law, holding that no amount of harm of discrimination can outweigh the speech interests of bigots, so long as they say something while doing it. Besides, if we restrict this, who knows where it will end. He is sure it will end with "Leda and the Swan." He did not suggest that bestiality statutes also had to go, along with obscenity's restrictions on depictions of sex between humans and animals. Both restrict a disapproved sexuality that, no doubt, contains an element of "mental intermediation."[46] Nothing in *Hudnut* explains why, if pornography is protected speech based on its mental elements, rape and sexual murder, which have mental elements, are not as well.

A dissent in a recent case invalidating sentence enhancements for crimes of bias could have been a dissent here: "The majority rationalizes their conclusion [that the statute violates the First Amendment] by insisting that this statute punishes bigoted thought. Not so. The statute does not impede or punish the right of persons to have bigoted thoughts or to express themselves in a bigoted fashion or otherwise, regarding the race, religion, or other status of a person. It does attempt to limit the effects of bigotry. What the statute does punish is acting upon those thoughts. It punishes the act of [discrimination] not the thought or expression of bigotry."[47]

Perhaps it is the nature of legal inequality that was missed by the Seventh Circuit. Discrimination has always been illegal because it is based on a prohibited motive: "an evil eye and an unequal hand,"[48] what the perpetrator is thinking while doing, what the acts mean. Racial classifications are thought illegal because they "supply a reason to infer antipathy."[49] A showing of discriminatory intent is required under the Fourteenth Amendment. Now we are told that this same motive, this same participation in a context of meaning, this same hatred and bigotry, these same purposes and thoughts, presumably this same intent, *protect* this same activity under the First Amendment. The courts cannot have it both ways, protecting discriminatory activity under the First Amendment on the same ground they make a requirement for its illegality under the Fourteenth. To put it another way, it is the "idea" of discrimination in the perpetrator's mind that courts have required be proven before the acts that effectuate it will be considered discriminatory. Surely, if acts that are otherwise legal, like hiring employees or renting rooms or admitting students, are made illegal under the Constitution by being based on race or sex because of what those who engage in them think about race or sex, acts that are otherwise *il*legal, like coercion, force, and assault, do not become constitutionally protected because they are done with the same thoughts in mind.

Seventh Circuit cases after *Hudnut* show that court attempting to straddle the fault lines beneath that decision without falling into an abyss. Some fancy footwork was required in a death penalty case[50] in which a sex murderer claimed he could not be held responsible for his actions because he was a lifelong pornography consumer. To receive the death penalty, a defendant must be capable of appreciating the wrongfulness of his actions, but that is exactly what pornography was proven to destroy in the consumer by evidence in this case. Noting that the *Hudnut* court had accepted the view that pornography perpetuates "subordination of women and violence against women" yet is protected because its harm depends on "mental intermediation," this panel, which included Judge Easterbrook, faced the dilemma *Hudnut* placed them in: "It would be impossible to hold both that pornography does not directly cause violence but criminal actors do, and that criminals do not cause violence, pornography does. The result would be to tell Indiana that it can neither ban pornography nor hold criminally responsible persons who are encouraged to commit violent acts because of pornography!"[51]

To get out of this, the court imagined that Indiana must have decided that rapists who are aware that a woman does not consent are not then excused by the rapists' belief that they have a right to proceed anyway. This is unsatisfying, as pornography makes rapists unaware that their victims are not consenting. As this record showed, it creates "a person who no longer distinguishes between violence and rape, or violence and sex."[52] There will, ultimately, be no way of addressing this problem short of changing the rape law so that it turns on what the perpetrator did rather than on what he thought *and* holding the pornographers jointly responsible for rapes they can be proven to have caused. Meantime, we kill a man rather than let his victims stop the pornography that produced him—leaving the pornographers completely off the hook. If anyone knows what they are doing, it is the pornographers.[53]

The nude dancing case the Supreme Court ultimately resolved came from the Seventh Circuit, where it produced eight separate opinions, the majority invalidating the regulation on First Amendment grounds. Judge Posner's concurrence turned Judge Easterbrook's protected "ideas" into protected "emotions," explaining that "[m]ost pornography is expressive, indeed expressive of the same emotions that a striptease expresses."[54] Since a videotape of nude dancing would be covered under the ordinance in *Hudnut,* and the ordinance in *Hudnut* restricted protected speech, he reasoned that nude dancing had to be protected speech as well: ". . . if this analysis is wrong, our decision in *Hudnut* is wrong."[55] The Supreme Court found the analysis was wrong. The regulation of nude dancing was valid under the First Amendment, even though striptease was not obscene. But Judge Posner was right about the connection between that case and protecting pornography as speech: their decision in *Hudnut* is wrong.

That these tortured consequences result from the lack of an equality context in which to interpret expressive freedoms is clear from the fact that the same issues produced exactly the opposite results in Canada. Canada's new constitution, the Charter of Rights and Freedoms,[56] includes an expansive equality guarantee and a serious entrenchment of freedom of expression. The Supreme Court of Canada's first move was to define equality in a meaningful way—one more substantive than formal, directed toward changing unequal social relations rather than monitoring their equal positioning before the law. The United States, by contrast, remains in the grip of what I affectionately call the stupid theory of equality. Inequality here is defined as distinction, as differentiation, indifferent to whether dominant or subordinated groups are hurt or helped. Canada, by contrast, following the argument of the Women's Legal Education and Action Fund (LEAF), repudiated this view in so many words, taking as its touchstone the treatment of historically disadvantaged groups and aiming to alter their status. The positive spin of the Canadian interpretation holds the law to promoting equality,[57] projecting the law into a more equal future, rather than remaining rigidly neutral in ways that either reinforce existing social inequality or prohibit changing it, as the American constitutional perspective has increasingly done in recent years.

The first case to confront expressive guarantees with equality requirements under the new constitution came in the case of James Keegstra, an anti-Semite who taught Holocaust revisionism to schoolchildren in Alberta. Prosecuted and convicted under Canada's hate propa-

ganda provision, Keegstra challenged the statute as a violation of the new freedom of expression guarantee.
LEAF intervened to argue that the hate propaganda law
promoted equality. We argued that group libel, most of
it concededly expression, promotes the disadvantage of
unequal groups; that group-based enmity, ill will, intolerance, and prejudice are the attitudinal engines of the
exclusion, denigration, and subordination that make up
and propel social inequality; that without bigotry, social systems of enforced separation, ghettoization, and
apartheid would be unnecessary, impossible, and unthinkable; that stereotyping and stigmatization of historically disadvantaged groups through group hate
propaganda shape their social image and reputation,
which controls their access to opportunities more pow-
erfully than their individual abilities ever do; and that it
is impossible for an individual to receive equality of opportunity when surrounded by an atmosphere of group
hate.

We argued that group defamation is a verbal form inequality takes, that just as white supremacy promotes inequality on the basis of race, color, and sometimes
ethnic or national origin, anti-Semitism promotes the
inequality of Jews on the basis of religion and ethnicity.
We argued that group defamation in this sense is not a
mere expression of opinion but a practice of discrimination in verbal form, a link in systemic discrimination

that keeps target groups in subordinated positions through the promotion of terror, intolerance, degradation, segregation, exclusion, vilification, violence, and genocide. We said that the nature of the practice can be understood and its impact measured from the damage it causes, from immediate psychic wounding to consequent physical aggression. Where advocacy of genocide is included in group defamation, we said an equality approach to such speech would observe that to be liquidated because of the group you belong to is the ultimate inequality.

The Supreme Court of Canada agreed with this approach, a majority upholding the hate propaganda provision, substantially on equality grounds. The Court recognized the provision as a content restriction—content that had to be stopped because of its antiegalitarian meaning and devastating consequences.[58]

Subsequently, the Winnipeg authorities arrested a whole pornography store and prosecuted the owner, Donald Victor Butler, for obscenity. Butler was convicted but said the obscenity law was an unconstitutional restriction on his Charter-based right of freedom of expression. LEAF argued that if Canada's obscenity statute, substantially different from U.S. obscenity law in prohibiting "undue exploitation of sex, or sex and violence, cruelty, horror, or crime," was interpreted to institutionalize some people's views about women and sex over others, it would be unconstitutional. But if the community standards applied were interpreted to prohibit harm to women as harm to the community, it was constitutional because it promoted sex equality.

The Supreme Court of Canada essentially agreed, upholding the obscenity provision on sex equality grounds.[59] It said that harm to women—which the Court was careful to make "contextually sensitive" and found could include humiliation, degradation, and subordination—*was* harm to society as a whole. The evidence on the harm of pornography was sufficient for a law against it. Violent materials always present this risk of harm, the Court said; explicit sexual materials that are degrading or dehumanizing (but not violent) could also unduly exploit sex under the obscenity provision if the risk of harm was substantial. Harm in this context was defined as "predispos[ing] persons to act in an anti-social manner, as, for example, the physical or mental mistreatment of women by men, or, what is perhaps debatable, the reverse." The unanimous Court noted that "if true equality between male and female persons is to be achieved, we cannot ignore the threat to equality resulting from exposure to audiences of certain types of violent and degrading material." The result rested in part on *Keegstra* but also observed that the harms attendant to the production of pornography situated the problem of pornography differently, such that the appearance of consent by women in such materials could exacerbate its injury. Recognizing that education could be helpful in combatting this harm, the court held that that fact did not make the provision unconstitutional.[60]

Although the Canadians considered the U.S. experience on these issues closely in both cases, the striking absence of a U.S.-style political speech litany suggests that taking equality seriously precludes it, or makes it look like the excuse for enforcing inequality that it has become. The decision did not mention the marketplace of ideas. Maybe in Canada, people talk to each other, rather than buy and sell each other as ideas. In an equality context, it becomes obvious that those with the most power buy the most speech, and that the marketplace rewards the powerful, whose views then become established as truth. We were not subjected to "Let [Truth] and falsehood grapple; who ever knew Truth put to the worse, in a free and open encounter." Milton had not been around for the success of the Big Lie technique, but this Court had.

Nor did the Canadian Court even consider the "slippery slope," a largely phony scruple impossible to sustain under a contextually sensitive equality rule. With inequality, the problem is not where intervention will end, but when it will ever begin. Equality is the law; if the slippery slope worked, the ineluctable logic of principle would have slid us into equality by now. Also, perhaps, because the Canadian law of equality is moored in the world, and knows the difference between disadvantaged groups and advantaged ones, it is less worried about the misfiring of restrictions against the powerless and more concerned about having nothing to fire against abuses of power by the powerful.

Fundamentally, the Supreme Court of Canada recognized the reality of inequality in the issues before it: this was not big bad state power jumping on poor powerless individual citizen, but a law passed to stand behind a comparatively powerless group in its social fight for equality against socially powerful and exploitative groups. This positioning of forces—which makes the hate propaganda prohibition and the obscenity law of Canada (properly interpreted) into equality laws, although neither was called such by Parliament—made the invocation of a tradition designed to keep government off the backs of people totally inappropriate. The Court also did not say that Parliament had to limit its efforts to stop the harm of inequality by talking to it. What it did was make more space for the unequal to find voice.

Nor did the Canadians intone, with Brandeis and nearly every American court that has ruled on a seriously contested speech issue since, that "[f]ear of serious injury cannot alone justify suppression of free speech ... Men feared witches and burnt women."[61] I have never understood this argument, other than as a way of saying that zealots misidentify the causes of their woes and hurt the wrong people. What has to be added to fear of serious injury to justify doing something about the speech that causes it? *Proof* of serious injury? If we can't restrict it then, when can we? Isn't fear of serious injury the concern behind restricting publication of the dates on which troop ships sail? Is it mere "fear" of injury to children that supports the law against the use of children to make pornography? If that isn't enough, why isn't proof of injury required? "Men feared witches and burnt women." Where is the speech here? Promoting the fear? Nobody tried to suppress tracts against witches. If somebody had, would some women not have been burnt? Or was it the witches' writings? Did they write? So burning their writings is part of the witch-hunt aspect of the fear? The women who are being burned as witches these days are the women in the pornography, and their burning is sex and entertainment and protected as speech. Those who are hunted down, stigmatized, excluded, and unpublished are the women who oppose their burning.

Neither Canadian decision reduces the harm of hate propaganda or pornography to its "offensiveness." When you hear the woman next door screaming as she is bounced off the walls by a man she lives with, are you "offended"? Hate speech and pornography do the same thing: enact the abuse. Women's reactions to the presentation of other women being sexually abused in pornography, and the reactions of Jews living in Skokie to having Nazis march through their town, are routinely trivialized in the United States as "being offended." The position of those with less power is equated with the position of those with more power, as if sexual epithets against straight white men were equivalent to sexual epithets against women, as if breaking the window of a Jewish-owned business in the world after Kristallnacht were just so much breaking glass.

In the cases both of pornography and of the Nazi march in Skokie, it is striking how the so-called speech reenacts the original experience of the abuse, and how its defense as speech does as well.[62] It is not only that both groups, through the so-called speech, are forcibly subjected to the spectacle of their abuse, legally legitimized. Both have their response to it trivialized as "being offended," that response then used to support its speech value, hence its legal protection.[63] Both are also told that what they can do about it is avert their eyes, lock their doors, stay home, stay silent, and hope the assault, and the animus it makes tangible, end when the film or the march ends. This is exactly what perpetrators of rape and child sexual abuse tell their victims and what the Jews in Germany were told by the Nazis (and the rest of the world) in the 1930s. Accept the freedom of your abusers. This best protects you in the end. Let it happen.

You are not really being hurt. When sexually abused women are told to let the system work and tolerate the pornography, this is what they are being told. The Jews in Germany, and the Jews in Skokie, were told to let the system work. At least this time around, the Jews of Canada were not, nor were sexually abused women.

The final absence in the Canadian decisions, perhaps the most startling, is the failure to mention any equivalent to the notion that, under the First Amendment, there is no such thing as a false idea. Perhaps under equality law, in some sense there is. When equality is recognized as a constitutional value and mandate, the idea that some people are inferior to others on the basis of group membership is authoritatively rejected as the basis for public policy. This does not mean that ideas to the contrary cannot be debated or expressed. It should mean, however, that social inferiority cannot be imposed through any means, including expressive ones.

Because society is made of language, distinguishing talk about inferiority from verbal imposition of inferiority may be complicated at the edges, but it is clear enough at the center with sexual and racial harassment, pornography, and hate propaganda. At the very least, when equality is taken seriously in expressive settings, such practices are not constitutionally insulated from regulation on the ground that the ideas they express cannot be regarded as false. Attempts to address them would not be prohibited—as they were in rejecting the Indianapolis pornography ordinance, for example—on the ground that, in taking a position in favor of equality, such attempts assume that the idea of human equality is true. The legal equality guarantee has already decided that. There is no requirement that the state remain neutral as between equality and inequality—quite the contrary. Equality is a "compelling state interest" that can already outweigh First Amendment rights in certain settings.[64] In other words, expressive means of practicing inequality can be prohibited.

This is not the place to spell out in detail all the policy implications of such a view. Suffice it to say that those who wish to keep materials that promote inequality from being imposed on students—such as academic books purporting to document women's biological inferiority to men, or arguing that slavery of Africans should return, or that Fourteenth Amendment equality should be repealed, or that reports of rape are routinely fabricated—especially without critical commentary, should not be legally precluded from trying on the grounds that the ideas contained in them cannot be assumed false. No teacher should be forced to teach falsehoods as if they must be considered provisionally true, just because bigots who have managed to get published have made their lies part of a debate. Teachers who wish to teach such materials should be prepared to explain what they are doing to avoid creating a hostile learning environment and to provide all students the equal benefit of an education. Wherever equality is mandated, racial and sexual epithets, vilification, and abuse should be able to be prohibited, unprotected by the First Amendment. The current legal distinction between screaming "go kill that nigger" and advocating the view that African-Americans should be eliminated from parts of the United States needs to be seriously reconsidered, if real equality is ever to be achieved. So, too, the current line separating pornography from hate speech and what is done to make pornography from the materials themselves.

Pornography, under current conditions, *is* largely its own context. Many believe that in settings that encourage critical distance, its showing does not damage women as much as it sensitizes viewers to the damage it does to women. My experience, as well as all the information available, makes me think that it is naive to believe that anything other words can do is as powerful as what pornography itself does. At the very least, pornography should never be imposed on a viewer who does not choose—then and there, without pressure of any kind—to be exposed to it. Tom Emerson said a long time ago that imposing what he called "erotic material" on individuals against their will is a form of action that "has all the characteristics of a physical assault."[65] Equality on campuses, in workplaces, everywhere, would be promoted if such assaults were actionable. Why any woman should have to attend school in a setting stacked against her equality by the showing of pornography—especially when authoritatively permitted by those who are legally obligated to take her equality seriously—is a question that those who support its showing should have to answer. The answer is not that she should have to wait for the resulting abuse or leave.

Where is all this leading? To a new model for freedom of expression in which the free speech position no longer supports social dominance, as it does now; in which free speech does not most readily protect the activities of Nazis, Klansmen, and pornographers, while doing nothing for their victims, as it does now; in which defending free speech is not speaking on behalf of a large pile of money in the hands of a small group of people, as it is now. In this new model, principle will be defined in terms of specific experiences, the particularity of history, substantively rather than abstractly. It will notice who is being hurt and never forget who they are. The state will have as great a role in providing relief from injury to equality through speech and in giving equal access to speech as it now has in disciplining its power to intervene in that speech that manages to get expressed.

In a society in which equality is a fact, not merely a word, words of racial or sexual assault and humiliation will be nonsense syllables. Sex between people and things, human beings and pieces of paper, real men and unreal women, will be a turn-off. Artifacts of these abuses will reside in a glass case next to the dinosaur skeletons in the Smithsonian. When this day comes, silence will be neither an act of power, as it is now for those who hide behind it, nor an experience of imposed powerlessness, as it is now for those who are submerged in it, but a context of repose into which thought can expand, an invitation that gives speech its shape, an opening to a new conversation.

NOTES

INDEX

NOTES

I. DEFAMATION AND DISCRIMINATION

1. Some of these facts are taken from years of confidential consultations with women who have been used in pornography; some are adapted from People v. Burnham, 222 Cal. Rptr. 630 (Ct. App. 1986), rev. denied, May 22, 1986, and media reports on it; and Norberg v. Wynrib [1992] 2 S.C.R. 224 (Can.).

2. Women used in pornography have provided the basis for the statements in these paragraphs over many years of work by me and my colleagues, including especially Andrea Dworkin, Therese Stanton, Evelina Giobbe, Susan Hunter, Margaret Baldwin, and Annie McCombs. Treatments of some of this damage are provided by Linda "Lovelace" and Michael McGrady, *Ordeal* (1980) (her experience of being coerced to make *Deep Throat*), and, in fiction, by Kathryn Harrison, *Exposures* (1993) (experience of child model for sex pictures by her father). See also Collette Marie, "The Coercion of Nudist Children," 3 *The ICONoclast* 1–6 (Spring 1991).

3. In the prosecution by Trish Crawford of South Carolina against her husband for marital rape, a thirty-minute videotape he took of the assault was shown. In it, Mr. Crawford has intercourse with her and penetrates her with objects while her hands and legs are tied with rope and her mouth is gagged and eyes blinded with duct tape. He was acquitted on a consent defense. "Acquittal of Husband Spurs Anger; Wife Accused of Raping Her," *Houston Chronicle,* April 18, 1992, sec. A, p. 3. The defendant testified he did not think his wife was serious when she said "no." Carolyn Pesce, "Marital Rape Case Acquittal Fuels Protest," *USA Today,* April 21, 1992, p. 3A. See also State v. Jean, 311 S.E.2d 266, 272–273 (N.C. 1984) (cross-examination of defendant on viewing pornographic movie five days after crime of rape charged, when movie showed the same kinds of sex acts charged, if error, was harmless).

4. As the defense lawyer in *Crawford* put it to the jury, as the tape described in note 3 above was played, "Was that a cry of pain and torture? Or was that a cry of pleasure?" "Marital Rape Acquittal Enrages Women's Groups," *Chicago Tribune,* April 18, 1992, p. 9C. This woman was clear she was being tortured. For the viewer who takes pleasure in her pain, however, the distinction between pain and pleasure does not exist. Her pain is his pleasure. This sexual sadism provides an incentive, even an epistemic basis, to impute pleasure to the victim as well. I believe this dynamic makes queries such as those by the defense lawyer successful in exonerating rapists.

5. In this setting, the only work regarded as part of the decon-

struction school that I have encountered that makes me hesitate even slightly in this characterization is Jean-François Lyotard, "The Differend, the Referent, and the Proper Name," 4 *diacritics* (Fall 1984). I read this work as an attack on the supposed difficulty of establishing that the Holocaust's gas chambers existed. It is, however, peculiar—and consistent with my critique here—that Lyotard does not mention that there are *Germans* who saw the gas chambers and survived to speak of their existence. His anatomy of silencing as a reality-disappearing device in its interconnection with the legal system is most useful, however. I am also unsure that this piece fits properly within deconstruction as a theoretical approach.

6. Andrea Dworkin's brilliant article on pornography infused new meaning into Woolf's phrase. Andrea Dworkin, "Against the Male Flood: Censorship, Pornography, and Equality," 8 *Harvard Women's Law Journal* 1 (1985).

7. Diana E. H. Russell, *The Secret Trauma* (1986) and *Rape in Marriage* (1990); United States Merit Protection Board, *Sexual Harassment of Federal Workers: Is It a Problem?* (1981); *Sexual Harassment of Federal Workers: An Update* (1988); Majority Staff of U.S. Senate Judiciary Committee, *Violence against Women: A Week in the Life of America* (1992).

8. For further discussion, see Andrea Dworkin, "Woman-Hating Right and Left," in J. Raymond and D. Leidholdt, eds., *The Sexual Liberals and the Attack on Feminism* (1990).

9. As to the state's position on pornography, American Book-

sellers Ass'n v. Hudnut, 771 F.2d 323 (7th Cir. 1985), aff'd, 475 U.S. 1001 (1986), makes explicit the protection of pornography that years of posturing and neglect under obscenity law left to interpretation.

10. See his opinion in Hudnut, 771 F.2d at 323.

11. Ronald Dworkin, "Pornography, Feminism, and Liberty," *New York Review of Books,* August 15, 1991.

12. Richard A. Posner, *Sex and Reason* (1992); Miller v. City of South Bend, 904 F.2d 1081, 1089–1104 (7th Cir. 1990) (Posner, J., concurring).

13. Edward DeGrazia, *Girls Lean Back Everywhere: The Law of Obscenity and the Assault on Genius* (1991).

14. I write about these issues in more detail in "Pornography as Defamation and Discrimination," 71 *Boston University Law Review* 793 (1991).

15. United States v. American Airlines, Inc., 743 F.2d 1114 (5th Cir. 1984), cert. dismissed, 474 U.S. 1001 (1985) ("highly verbal crime," 1121; "Raise your goddamn . . ." and "We can talk about any . . ." are both on 1116).

16. Palmer v. Thompson, 403 U.S. 217 (1971) (holding that closure by city of Jackson, Mississippi, of public swimming pools formerly available to "whites only" did not violate equal protection clause of the Fourteenth Amendment because both Blacks and whites were denied access); Jones v. Alfred H. Mayer Co., 392 U.S. 409 (1968) (prohibiting discriminatory sale or rental of property to "whites only"); Blow v. North Carolina, 379 U.S. 684 (1965) (holding that restaurant serving "whites only" violated Civil Rights Act

of 1964); Watson v. City of Memphis, 373 U.S. 526 (1963) (holding that city's operation of large percentage of publicly owned recreational facilities for "whites only" due to delays in implementing desegregation violated the Fourteenth Amendment); see also Hazelwood Sch. Dist. v. United States, 433 U.S. 299, 304–305 n.7 (1977) (stating that, in employment discrimination claim against school district, plaintiffs alleged that district's newspaper advertisement for teacher applicants specified "white only"); Pierson v. Ray, 386 U.S. 547, 558 (1967) (holding that Black and white clergymen did not consent to their arrest by peacefully entering the "White Only" designated waiting area of bus terminal).

17. *The Yellow Spot: The Outlawing of Half a Million Human Beings* 176–177 (1936) (photos of "Jews not wanted" signs).

18. Pittsburgh Press Co. v. Pittsburgh Comm'n on Human Relations, 413 U.S. 376, 379 (1973) ("help wanted—male"); Alexander v. Yale Univ., 459 F. Supp. 1, 3–4 (D. Conn. 1977), aff'd, 631 F.2d 178 (2d Cir. 1984) (offer of "A" grade for sexual compliance); Stockett v. Tolin, 791 F. Supp. 1536, 1543 (S.D. Fla. 1992) ("F—— me or you're fired"); Hopkins v. Price Waterhouse, 825 F.2d 458, 463 (D.C. Cir. 1987) ("walk more femininely..."); Davis v. Passman, 442 U.S. 228, 230 (1979) ("...be a man").

19. State v. Davidson, 481 N.W.2d 51, 59 (Minn. 1992).

20. The law actually appears to permit the regulation of some forms of expression that manipulate the mind without its

conscious awareness. Subliminal communications are flatly prohibited as "deceptive" in the advertising of distilled spirits. 27 C.F.R. §5.65(h) (1992). The National Association of Broadcasters favors regulation of subliminal communication; its voluntary guidelines were invalidated on antitrust grounds, United States v. National Ass'n of Broadcasters, 536 F. Supp. 149 (D.D.C. 1982).

The most evocative and advanced treatment of the issue occurs in Vance v. Judas Priest, 1990 WL 130920 (Nev. Dist. Ct. Aug. 24, 1990). Two boys attempted suicide, one successfully, as a result, it was alleged, of messages embedded in a heavy metal recording. The court found the subliminals not to be protected by the First Amendment based on a right to be free of intrusive speech, because subliminal communications do not advance the purposes of free speech, and because of the listeners' right to privacy. The court also found no proximate cause existed between the lyrics and the suicides. NBC, CBS, and ABC all have policies prohibiting subliminal messages in ads, but I could find none regarding program content. See generally T. Bliss, "Subliminal Projection: History and Analysis," 5 *Comment* 419, 422 (1983); Wilson Key, *Subliminal Seduction* (1972); Scot Silverglate, Comment, "Subliminal Perception and the First Amendment: Yelling Fire in a Crowded Mind," 44 *University of Miami Law Review* 1243 (1990).

21. Hudnut, 771 F.2d at 328–329.

22. This does not mean that all masturbation material is

pornography. Nor is this a definition; it is an empirical observation.

23. Aristotle, *Nicomachean Ethics*, as cited in Posner, *Sex and Reason* at 1.

24. "Wenn der putz stegt, ligt der seykhel in drerd" is the best transliteration I could find, thanks to Alan Keiler.

25. Schiro v. Clark, 963 F.2d 962, 972 (7th Cir. 1992), cert. granted, May 17, 1993 (No. 92–7549). See fuller description in III.

26. Hudnut, 771 F.2d at 329.

27. Documentation of the harm of pornography in real life is contained in Public Hearings on Ordinances to Add Pornography as Discrimination against Women, Minneapolis City Council, Government Operations Committee (Dec. 12 and 13, 1983); M. McManus, ed., *Final Report of the Attorney General's Commission on Pornography* (1986); *Pornography and Prostitution in Canada: Report of the Special Committees on Pornography and Prostitution* (1985). See also Diana E. H. Russell, "Pornography and Rape: A Causal Model," 9 *Political Psychology* 41 (1988); Gloria Cowan et al., "Dominance and Inequality in X-Rated Videocassettes," 12 *Psychology of Women Quarterly* 299, 306–307 (1988); Park E. Dietz and Alan E. Sears, "Pornography and Obscenity Sold in Adult Bookstores: A Survey of 5,132 Books, Magazines, and Films in Four American Cities," 21 *University of Michigan Journal of Law Reform* 7, 38–43 (1987–88) (documenting violence, bondage, sadomasochism, and gender differences in

pornography); Neil M. Malamuth and Barry Spinner, "A Longitudinal Content Analysis of Sexual Violence in the Best-Selling Erotic Magazines," 16 *Journal of Sexual Research* 226–227 (1980) (documenting increases in violent sex in pornography).

28. In addition to the citations in the preceding note, my own five years of research on the making of pornography in cults and white supremacist organizations, for marketing by organized crime, informs this paragraph.

29. When women are coerced to perform for pornography, the resulting materials should clearly be actionable in spite of Simon & Schuster, Inc. v. Members of the New York State Crime Victims Bd., 112 S. Ct. 501 (1991), which invalidated a statutory financial restriction on books that were products of criminal activity. Most centrally, the crimes considered by the *Simon & Schuster* court were not committed so that they could be written about. The court also recognized that the state "has an undisputed compelling interest in ensuring that criminals do not profit from their crimes," 510, which may be pursued by narrowly tailored means.

30. Under the recent decision holding a magazine publisher liable for a murder that resulted from an ad it ran, the consequential coercion produced by coerced pornography may be at least as "foreseeable," especially if the coercion is visible in the materials. Braun v. Soldier of Fortune Magazine, Inc., 968 F.2d 1110, 1118 (11th Cir. 1992) (negligence standard that ad "'on its face' would have alerted a reasonably prudent publisher that [it] 'contained a clearly

identifiable unreasonable risk that the offer . . . is one to commit a serious violent crime'" satisfies First Amendment).

31. J. L. Austin's *How to Do Things with Words* (1962) is the original enunciation of the theory of performative speech, which examines language for which "the issuing of the utterance is the performing of an action—it is not normally thought of as just saying something," at 6–7. While he does not confine himself to inequality, which is crucial to my argument here, neither does he generalize the performative to all speech, as have many speech act theorists who came after him. Austin is less an authority for my particular development of "doing things with words" and more a foundational exploration of the view in language theory that some speech can be action.

32. For discussion, see Andrea Dworkin and Catharine A. MacKinnon, *Pornography and Civil Rights: A New Day for Women's Equality* (1988). The Model Ordinance, making pornography actionable as a civil rights violation, defines "pornography" as "the graphic sexually explicit subordination of women through pictures and/or words that also includes one or more of the following: (a) women are presented dehumanized as sexual objects, things, or commodities; or (b) women are presented as sexual objects who enjoy humiliation or pain; or (c) women are presented as sexual objects experiencing sexual pleasure in rape, incest, or other sexual assault; or (d) women are presented as sexual objects tied up or cut up or mutilated or bruised or physically hurt; or (e) women are presented in

postures or positions of sexual submission, servility, or display; or (f) women's body parts—including but not limited to vaginas, breasts, or buttocks—are exhibited such that women are reduced to those parts; or (g) women are presented being penetrated by objects or animals; or (h) women are presented in scenarios of degradation, humiliation, injury, torture, shown as filthy or inferior, bleeding, bruised, or hurt in a context that makes these conditions sexual." In this definition, the use of "men, children, or transsexuals in the place of women" is also pornography.

33. Query whether all elements of speech are necessarily either "content" or "noncontent."

34. New York v. Ferber, 458 U.S. 747, 763 (1982), cited in R.A.V. v. City of St. Paul, 112 S. Ct. 2538, 2543 (1992).

35. Osborne v. Ohio, 495 U.S. 103, 111 (1990) (use of child pornography by pedophiles may hurt children other than those in it).

36. Creel Froman, *Language and Power* 112 (1992).

37. Olivia N. v. National Broadcasting Co., 141 Cal. Rptr. 511, 512 (1977), cert. denied sub nom. Niemi v. National Broadcasting Co., 458 U.S. 1108 (1982) ("The complaint alleges that the assailants had seen the 'artificial rape' scene" on television).

38. This more sophisticated version is illustrated by Susanne Kappeler, *The Pornography of Representation* (1986).

39. "What matters for a legal system is what words *do,* not what they *say* . . ." Edward J. Bloustein, "Holmes: His First

Amendment Theory and His Pragmatist Bent," 40 *Rutgers Law Review* 283, 299 (1988).

40. Personnel Administrator v. Feeney, 442 U.S. 256 (1979); Washington v. Davis, 426 U.S. 229 (1976).

41. Postmodernism is premodern in the sense that it cannot grasp, or has forgotten, or is predicated on obscuring, this function of language in social hierarchy.

42. Barnes v. Glen Theatre, 111 S. Ct. 2456, 2466 n.4 (1991) ("Nudity is *not* normally engaged in for the purpose of communicating an idea or an emotion"). But see Schad v. Borough of Mt. Ephraim, 452 U.S. 61, 66 (1981) (suggesting that nude dancing has some protection from regulation).

43. *Barnes v. Glen Theatre* was litigated below as Miller v. City of South Bend, 904 F.2d 1081, 1131 (7th Cir. 1990) ("At oral argument Miller's attorney admitted that this dancing communicated no idea or message").

44. Brief for Appellants at 5–6, California v. LaRue, 409 U.S. 109 (1972) (No. 71–36) (in nude dancing establishment, oral copulation of women by customers, masturbation by customers, inserting money from customers into vagina, rubbing money on vaginal area, customers with rolled-up currency in mouths placing same in women's vaginas, customers using flashlights rented by licensees to better observe women's genitalia, customers placing dollar bills on bar and women attempting to squat and pick up bills with labia, women urinating in beer glasses and giving them back to customer, women sitting on bars and placing their

legs around customers' heads, etc.). See also Common-
wealth v. Kocinski, 414 N.E.2d 378 (Mass. App. Ct. 1981).

45. Barnes, 111 S. Ct. at 2468–71 (interest in preventing prostitution, sexual assault, and other attendant harms sufficient to support nude dancing provision). See also the
extensive discussion of these harms in the dissenting opinion by Judge Coffey in Miller, 904 F.2d at 1104–20.

46. Barnes, 111 S. Ct. at 2458 (Rehnquist) and 2471 (Souter).

47. Ibid. at 2468.

48. These examples are discussed and documented in a brief
by Burke Marshall and me, Brief Amicus Curiae of the National Black Women's Health Project, R.A.V. v. City of St.
Paul, 112 S. Ct. 2538 (1992) (No. 90–7675).

49. R.A.V., 112 S. Ct. at 2547.

50. Ibid. at 2569.

51. Andrea Dworkin and I discuss this in our *Pornography and
Civil Rights: A New Day for Women's Equality* 60–61
(1988).

52. James R. McGovern, *Anatomy of a Lynching* 84 (1982).

53. An incident in Los Angeles in which a Black man was photographed being beaten by police who were acquitted in a
criminal trial after repeated showings to the jury of a
videotape of the assaults makes me think there is more to
this than I thought. Two of the officers were later convicted in a civil trial.

54. A recent legal defense of the White Aryan Resistance, and
its leaders Tom and John Metzger, connected with the
murder of an African man in part through a leaflet orga-
nizing skinheads to kill Blacks in "Aryan" race-destined
territory, suggests this: because the murder was effectuated

through a leaflet with a political ideology, it was not plain old advocacy to commit murder, it was *bigoted* advocacy to commit murder *in writing*—hence protected expression. See Berhanu v. Metzger, 119 Ore. App. 175, (No. CA A67833), Appellants' Opening Brief (Jan. 29, 1992). The defendants' conviction for wrongful death, conspiracy, and murder by agency, with damages, has been upheld over First Amendment challenge. Berhanu v. Metzger, 119 Ore. App. 175 (April 14, 1993).

55. Brockett v. Spokane Arcades, Inc., 472 U.S. 491, 503 n.12 (1985), appears to refer to child pornography as an issue of "pure speech rather than conduct."

56. Brief on Behalf of American Booksellers Ass'n et al., New York v. Ferber, 458 U.S. 747 (1982) (No. 81-55).

57. Ferber, 458 U.S. at 747.

58. Osborne v. Ohio, 495 U.S. 103, 111 (1990). This harm seems to have been lost sight of in the recent ruling in United States v. X-Citement Video, Inc., 982 F.2d 1285 (9th Cir. 1992), in which the majority allows downstream vendors of child pornography to use their lack of knowledge of a child's actual age as a defense. The dissent recognizes the harm to those who are "hurt by the attitudes these materials foster." X-Citement Video, 982 F.2d at 1293–94 n.3 (Kozinski, J., dissenting).

59. Stanley v. Georgia, 394 U.S. 557, 568 n.11 (1969).

60. 16 *Penthouse* 118 (December 1984).

61. Robinson v. Jacksonville Shipyards, Inc., 760 F. Supp. 1486 (M.D. Fla. 1991).

62. George Fisher was convicted of the murder and attempted rape of Jean Kar-Har Fewel, an eight-year-old adopted

Chinese girl found strangled to death hanging from a tree in 1985. Mr. Fisher testified that he went to an adult bookstore on the day of the murder to watch movies. UPI, August 20, 1985.

63. Hudnut, 771 F.2d at 328.

64. This is, in effect, what is permitted in Herceg v. Hustler Magazine, Inc., 814 F.2d 1017 (5th Cir. 1987) (survivors of boy who died of autoerotic asphyxia may not recover against *Hustler,* which caused it).

65. Hudnut, 771 F.2d at 328–329.

66. Ibid. at 329–331.

67. Gitlow v. New York, 268 U.S. 652, 673 (1925) (Holmes, J., dissenting).

68. For a discussion of how "pornographers are more like the police in police states," see Andrea Dworkin, "Against the Male Flood," in *Letters from a War Zone* 264 (1988).

69. For an analysis of the place of pornography in male power, see Andrea Dworkin, *Pornography: Men Possessing Women* 13–47 (1979).

70. Andrea Dworkin has said this in many public speeches, including ones I attended in 1983 and 1984. The idea behind it was originally developed in her *Pornography: Men Possessing Women* at 48–100.

71. Andrea Dworkin, *Intercourse* 194 (1987).

II. RACIAL AND SEXUAL HARASSMENT

1. Brooms v. Regal Tube Co., 881 F.2d 412, 416, 417 (7th Cir. 1989).

2. Morgan v. Hertz Corp., 542 F. Supp. 123, 128 (W.D. Tenn.

1981), aff'd sub nom. Sones-Morgan v. Hertz Corp., 725
F.2d 1070 (6th Cir. 1984). See also Snell v. Suffolk County,
611 F. Supp. 521, 525 (E.D.N.Y. 1985), aff'd, 782 F.2d 1094
(2d Cir. 1986). The first commentator to show alarm is
Kingsley R. Browne, "Title VII as Censorship: Hostile-
Environment Harassment and the First Amendment," 52
Ohio State Law Journal 481 (1991). See also Amy Horton,
Comment, "Of Supervision, Centerfolds, and Censorship:
Sexual Harassment, the First Amendment, and the Con-
tours of Title VII," 46 *University of Miami Law Review* 403
(1991).

3. Davis v. Monsanto Chem. Co., 858 F.2d 345, 350 (6th Cir.
1988) (racist abuse found insufficient to make out hostile
environment). This approach includes a recent case of
racial harassment in which an injunction directed defendant to "cease . . . any policy . . . or activity . . . which
perpetuates [or] condones . . . racial harassment . . . including . . . any and all offensive conduct and speech impli-
cating considerations of race." Harris v. International
Paper Co., 765 F. Supp. 1509, 1527 (D. Me. 1991). A par-
tial exception is one case which summarily rejected a First
Amendment defense, Jew v. University of Iowa, 749 F.
Supp. 946, 961 (S.D. Iowa 1990).

4. See discussion in I, pages 31–33.

5. Hall v. Gus Constr. Co., 842 F.2d 1010, 1012 (8th Cir.
1988) ("Cavern Cunt"); Moffett v. Gene B. Glick Co., 621
F. Supp. 244, 253–255 (N.D. Ind. 1985) ("stupid cunt");
Branda v. Sanford, 637 P.2d 1223, 1224 (Nev. 1981)
("fucking cunt"); Reynolds v. Atlantic City Convention
Ctr., 53 Fair Empl. Prac. Cas. (BNA) 1852, 1856 (D.N.J.

1990), aff'd, 905 F.2d 419 (3d Cir. 1991) (repeated use of word "cunt"). A woman worker who was referred to by a co-worker as a "cunt" could present a strong case for sexual harassment; Rabidue v. Osceola Refining Co., 805 F.2d 611, 624–628 (Keith, J., concurring in part, dissenting in part), cert. denied, 481 U.S. 1041 (1987).

6. Savage and Dep't of Corrections, 37 Ill. H.R. Comm. Rpts. 320, 340 (1988).

7. Robinson v. Jacksonville Shipyards, Inc., 760 F. Supp. 1486, 1497 (M.D. Fla. 1991) (dartboard); testimony to press on Minneapolis ordinance on pornography, 1984 (construction site). See also Lipsett v. University of Puerto Rico, 864 F.2d 881, 888 (1st Cir. 1988) (walls of rest facility plastered with pornography).

8. Morris v. American Nat'l Can Co., 730 F. Supp. 1489, 1490 (E.D. Mo. 1989) ("spit or swallow"); Robinson, 760 F. Supp. at 1495, 1498 (all the rest).

9. These facts are taken from a case on which I worked in Ontario, Canada.

10. Department of Fair Empl. & Hous. v. Livermore Joe's, Inc., Cal FEHC Dec. 90–07 (1990).

11. Zabkowicz v. West Bend Co., 589 F. Supp. 780, 782 (E.D. Wis. 1984).

12. "9 to 5, 1992 National Boss Conte Cleveland," PR Newswire, March 12, 1992.

13. Walker v. Ford Motor Co., 684 F.2d 1355, 1358–59 (11th Cir. 1982).

14. A computer search of federal sexual and racial harassment cases through 1992 yields 144 cases that involve alleged jokes. Usually the courts are not laughing. Sometimes, if

the woman jokes back, she is regarded as participating, hence not harassed. Sexual jokes formed a substantial part of a successful complaint for constructive discharge in Martin v. City of Youngstown, 961 F.2d 1578 (6th Cir. April 28, 1992) (text in Westlaw), cert. denied sub nom. City of Youngstown v. Martin, 113 S. Ct. 813 (1992). For a superb discussion of racial "jokes," see Snell, 611 F. Supp. at 529–530.

15. Meritor Savings Bank v. Vinson, 477 U.S. 57 (1986).

16. "Sexual expression which is indecent but not obscene is protected by the First Amendment . . ." Sable Communications v. FCC, 492 U.S. 115, 126 (1989). In another case, involving a licensing scheme for "adult" establishments, the city conceded that sexually explicit speech was protected by the First Amendment. FW/PBS v. City of Dallas, 493 U.S. 215, 224 (1990) (O'Connor, J., for the plurality).

17. The leading case of Rogers v. EEOC, 454 F.2d 234 (5th Cir. 1971), cert. denied, 406 U.S. 957 (1972), which inferred an atmosphere of discrimination against nurses from the segregation of patients on the basis of ethnicity, does not mention speech as a concern, nor do any of the hundreds of cases brought for similar injuries since which have been based on verbal acts.

18. Harris, 765 F. Supp. at 1518 and many many cases.

19. Walker, 684 F.2d at 1359.

20. Vance v. Southern Bell Tel. & Tel. Co., 863 F.2d 1503, 1506 (11th Cir. 1989); Hunter v. Allis-Chalmers Corp., 797 F.2d 1417, 1420 (7th Cir. 1986).

21. Cited in Mary Ellen Gale, "On Curbing Racial Speech," *The Responsive Community* 47 (Winter 1990/1991).

22. See discussion in I, page 30, and III, pages 94–95.

23. This point is supported by Laurence Tribe, "Does the Constitution Prevent Enhanced Sentencing for 'Hate Crimes'?" Testimony before the Subcommittee on Crime and Criminal Justice on H.R. 4797 (Hate Crimes Sentencing Enhancement Act of 1992), July 29, 1992.

24. Rabidue, 805 F.2d at 620–622.

25. Reynolds, 53 Fair Empl. Prac. Cas. (BNA) at 1886.

26. Snell, 611 F. Supp. at 528. While the court that ruled that women must tolerate pornography at work did not mention the First Amendment (Rabidue, 805 F.2d at 611), one court that held racist abuse actionable expressly held, without elaboration, that "the First Amendment does not bar appropriate relief in the instant case of discrimination in the workplace." Snell, 611 F. Supp. at 531.

27. Bennett v. N.Y. City Dep't of Corrections, 705 F. Supp. 979, 986 (S.D.N.Y. 1989) (fact prisons are '"coarse and rowdy' . . . does not mean that anything goes"); Barbetta v. Chemlawn Servs. Co., 669 F. Supp. 569, 573 n.2 (W.D.N.Y. 1987), rejects *Rabidue,* as do Robinson, 760 F. Supp. at 1525, and Ellison v. Brady, 924 F.2d 872, 877 (9th Cir. 1991).

28. The University of Wisconsin policy on discriminatory harassment was limited to abuse "directed at" individuals, but this did not save it; UMW Post, Inc. v. Board of Regents, 774 F. Supp. 1163, 1172 (D. Wis. 1991). The ACLU's policy on sexual harassment, while it does not mention speech concerns at all, is centered on quid pro quo harassment, and restricts the hostile environment type to that

"where a pattern and practice of sexual conduct or expression is directed at a specific employee and has definable consequences for the individual victim ..." ACLU Policy #316 at (6), Board Minutes, April 14–15, 1984, June 23–24, 1984. The ACLU argued to the same effect in Lois Robinson's case, Brief for Amicus Curiae, American Civil Liberties Union Found. of Florida, Inc. and American Civil Liberties Union, Inc. at 14–17, Robinson v. Jacksonville Shipyards, Inc. (11th Cir. 1993) (No. 91–3655). The brief terms this sign "speech or other expressive activity." The most extended treatment of this distinction to date can be found in Eugene Volokh, "Freedom of Speech and Workplace Harassment," 39 *UCLA Law Review* 1791, 1868 (1992).

29. The state's brief in *Beauharnais v. Illinois* opposed this distinction in exactly these terms: "petitioner cannot gain constitutional protection from the consequence of libel by multiplying victims and identifying them by a collective term." Respondent's Brief, Beauharnais v. Illinois, 343 U.S. 250 (1952) (No. 118) at 4. While Illinois won that round, the law of group libel has since developed in precisely this direction.

Another part of the idea is that an environment can hurt only the individual engaged in the direct sexual byplay but cannot hurt those not so involved, even if they are surrounded by it, perhaps even if it determines their job opportunities. Waltman v. International Paper Co., 875 F.2d 468, 482–486 (Jones, J., dissenting). But cf. Broderick v. Ruder, 685 F. Supp. 1269 (D.D.C. 1988); King v. Palmer,

778 F.2d 878 (D.C. Cir. 1985); 29 C.F.R. §1604.11(g) (employer preference for female employees who submit to sex can constitute sexual harassment of other female employees).

30. An example like this was litigated in Snell, 611 F. Supp. at 525 ("Official Runnin' Nigger Target" with bullet holes, Exhibit 13).

31. Brief of ACLU, note 28 above at 11–12. Robinson, 760 F. Supp. at 1495–98.

32. Post, 774 F. Supp. at 1168.

33. Catharine A. MacKinnon, Testimony on S. 1484 Labor and Human Resources Committee (Sept. 19, 1992), 36 *Law Quadrangle Notes* 25 (1993). Examples not otherwise annotated in this paragraph are from Gale, "On Curbing Racial Speech" at 47.

34. See generally Mari J. Matsuda, "Public Response to Racist Speech: Considering the Victim's Story," 87 *Michigan Law Review* 2320 (1989).

35. An obvious example is NLRB v. Gissel Packing Co., 395 U.S. 575 (1969) (threatening employer speech that was unfair labor practice was not protected speech).

36. Robinson, 760 F. Supp. at 1486, is the leading case on pornography as sexual harassment. Rabidue, 805 F.2d at 611, disallows a Title VII claim based substantially on pornography, but not for reasons of protecting it as speech.

37. Post, 774 F. Supp. at 1163; Doe v. University of Michigan, 721 F. Supp. 852 (E.D. Mich. 1989).

38. It is arguable that all misogyny is fundamentally sexual, systemically speaking. It does not always express itself in explicitly sexual ways, however.

39. Robinson, 760 F. Supp. at 1498.

40. Ibid.

41. Morris, 730 F. Supp. at 1489.

42. Weiss v. United States, 595 F. Supp. 1050, 1053 (E.D. Va. 1984).

43. I saw this epithet most recently in an elevator at Yale Law School in 1990.

44. EEOC v. Murphy Motor Freight Lines, Inc., 488 F. Supp. 381, 384 (D. Minn. 1980).

45. See Carter v. Sedgwick County, 705 F. Supp. 1474, 1476 (D. Kan. 1988), aff'd in part, vacated in part, rev'd in part, 929 F.2d 1501 (10th Cir. 1991).

46. Beauharnais v. Illinois, 343 U.S. 250, 251 (1952).

47. Regina v. McCraw, [1991] 66 C.C.C. (3d) 517, 519–520 (Can.): "Each letter was personally addressed to one of the three cheerleaders. The letters are so similar that it is sufficient for the purpose of these reasons to set out the contents of one of them:

"Sandy

"Let me tell you, your [*sic*] a beautiful woman, I am disapointed [*sic*] you wernt [*sic*] in the calendar, you are the most beautiful cheerleader on the squad. I think you should pose nude for playboy. Every time I see you I get an instant erection. I masturbate thinking about you every night. Fucking you would be like a dream come true. I would lick your whole body, starting with your toes, up your legs, then right to your vagina. I would love to taste your juicy vagina. Then I would suck on your perfect, well shaped breasts, I would then turn you over and lick your asshole. Then you would go down and suck my dick. Once I am nice and horny, I would stick my dick in your vagina. Then I would shove my dick into your nice tight asshole. Then you would suck my dick, and I would shoot my sperm all over your face. I am going to fuck you even if I have to *rape* you. Even if it takes me till the day I die. There should be more beautiful woman [*sic*] around like you.

"See you later and have a nice day!"

48. An interesting discussion of the sexual, gendered, and contextual dimension of such terms can be found in Savage and Dep't of Corrections, 37 Ill. H.R. Comm. Rpts. 320 (1988).

49. Robinson, 760 F. Supp. at 1498.

50. Jacobo Timerman, *Prisoner without a Name, Cell without a Number* 60–80 (1981).

51. This is what employer Sidney Taylor said to Mechelle Vinson as he raped her repeatedly in a motel, Brief of Respondent at 30, Meritor Savings Bank v. Vinson, 477 U.S. 57 (1986) (No. 84–1979).

52. I was surprised to discover, at the end of an extensive literature search, that no laboratory or experimental research on racist hate literature exists parallel to that on the effects of exposure to pornography. This is not to suggest that the Holocaust or the U.S. experience with lynching or with

racism in general, provides an insufficient body of evidence on its effects.

53. Hearings on the Clarence Thomas Supreme Court Nomination before the Senate Committee on the Judiciary, Federal News Service, October 11, 1991, available in LEXIS, Nexis Library, FEDNEW File.

54. Patricia J. Williams, "A Rare Case Study of Muleheadedness and Men," in Toni Morrison, ed., *Race-ing Justice, Engendering Power: Essays on Anita Hill, Clarence Thomas, and the Construction of Social Reality* 169 (1992).

55. According to my notes from that period, these words were uttered in the media in commentary on Anita Hill's testimony, President Bush and Senator Grassley on national television shows, Deborah Norville on her radio show, in October 1991.

III. EQUALITY AND SPEECH

1. Of course, the modern doctrine of free speech technically relies on the Fourteenth Amendment to apply its prohibition of government censorship to the states, without involving the equality guarantee at all. Modern speech doctrine dates from Masses Pub. Co. v. Patten, 244 F. 535 (S.D.N.Y. 1917), rev'd, 246 F. 24 (2d Cir. 1917); Schenck v. United States, 249 U.S. 47 (1919); and Abrams v. United States, 250 U.S. 616 (1919) (especially the dissent of Justice Holmes).

2. As the Court put it, "necessarily . . . under the Equal Pro-

tection Clause, not to mention the First Amendment itself, government may not grant the use of a forum to people whose views it finds acceptable, but deny it to those wishing to express less favored or more controversial views." Police Department v. Mosley, 408 U.S. 92, 96 (1972). Some possible implications of these cases are discussed in a seminal article by Kenneth L. Karst, "Equality as a Central Principle in the First Amendment," 43 *University of Chicago Law Review* 20 (1975). While the article notes that "the relation between formal and substantive equality" is raised by these speech cases decided on equal protection grounds (p. 22), it does not discuss this issue in any depth, nor does it see any tension between existing First Amendment approaches and the trajectory of the equality principle.

3. Access problems are better recognized, for example, in the broadcast area than are the damage issues anywhere. On access, see Karst, "Equality as a Central Principle" note 2 above; Thomas I. Emerson, "The Affirmative Side of the First Amendment," 15 *Georgia Law Review* 795 (1981); Red Lion Broadcasting Co. v. FCC, 395 U.S. 367 (1969). A particularly pertinent discussion is Metro Broadcasting, Inc. v. FCC, 497 U.S. 547 (1990), in which a narrow Supreme Court majority upheld minority preferences in "distress sales" of radio or television broadcast licenses, in part on a rationale of promoting greater programming diversity. But cf. Lamprecht v. FCC, 958 F.2d 382 (D.C. Cir. 1992) (preferences for women owners of radio station vio-

late equal protection). See also the perceptive opinion of Justice O'Connor on the implications of expressive association in Roberts v. United States Jaycees, 468 U.S. 609, 631 (1984) (O'Connor, J., concurring).

4. See II, notes 31 and 32; and R.A.V. v. City of St. Paul, 112 S. Ct. 2538 (1992); Doe v. University of Michigan, 721 F. Supp. 852 (E.D. Mich. 1989); UMW Post, Inc. v. Board of Regents, 774 F. Supp. 1163 (E.D. Wis. 1991).

5. Thus Kalven treating problems raised by "the Negro" for the First Amendment in 1965 does not mention education. Harry Kalven, Jr., *The Negro and the First Amendment* (1965).

6. "The Congress shall have power to enforce, by appropriate legislation, the provisions of this article." U.S. Const. amend. XIV, §5. See also Catharine A. MacKinnon, "Reflections on Sex Equality under Law," 100 *Yale Law Journal* 1281, 1283 n.12 (1991).

7. A further possible result is that escalations of hate propaganda and pornography, as for example in Eastern Europe, will be met with indifference or embraced as freedom under U.S.-style speech theory. As pornography and its defense as "speech" take over more of the world, pervading law and consciousness, desensitizing populations to inhumanity, and sexualizing inequality, there are grounds for concern that legal attempts to reverse rising racial, ethnic, and religious discrimination, harassment, and aggression will be disabled.

8. The origin of this notion appears to be "The best test of

truth is the power of the thought to get itself accepted in the competition of the market." Abrams, 250 U.S. 616 at 630 (Holmes, J., dissenting).

9. John Milton, *Areopagitica* 58 (Richard Jebb ed., 1918): "Let [Truth] and falsehood grapple; who ever knew Truth put to the worse, in a free and open encounter?"

10. See a wonderful critical article by Fred Schauer, "Slippery Slopes," 99 *Harvard Law Review* 361 (1985).

11. This, of course, is not the real law of the First Amendment, which makes judgments as to content all the time.

12. The authoritative articulation of this notion is in a defamation case, Gertz v. Robert Welch, Inc., 418 U.S. 323, 339–340 (1974): "Under the First Amendment there is no such thing as a false idea. However pernicious an opinion may seem, we depend for its correction not on the conscience of judges and juries but on the competition of other ideas." While the second sentence suggests that the marketplace of ideas, not courts, is the forum for rectifying false opinions, the Court has refused to recognize a special exemption from defamation actions "for anything that might be labeled 'opinion . . .'" Milkovich v. Lorain Journal Co., 497 U.S. 1, 18 (1990). The Court also stated that "the fair meaning of the [*Gertz*] passage is to equate the word 'opinion' in the second sentence with the word 'idea' in the first sentence," suggesting that while ideas should be corrected by other ideas, there is no blanket protection from libel actions based on "anything that might be labeled 'opinion.'" Milkovich, 497 U.S. at 18.

13. Cohen v. California, 403 U.S. 15 (1971). "Offensive" is a

word used to describe obscenity. Paris Adult Theatre I v. Slaton, 413 U.S. 49, 71 (1973) (Douglas, J., dissenting) ("'Obscenity' at most is the expression of offensive ideas"). Indeed, "patently offensive" is an element of the obscenity test. Miller v. California, 413 U.S. 15, 24 (1973).

14. Erznoznik v. City of Jacksonville, 422 U.S. 205, 212 (1975).

15. It is my observation that anyone who attended primary school anywhere but in the United States tends to regard this approach, and the passion with which it is defended, as an American cultural peculiarity or fetish to be tolerated. That the United States fails to ratify various international treaties because of this oddity is viewed with somewhat less affection. Mari J. Matsuda, "Public Response to Racist Speech: Considering the Victim's Story," 87 *Michigan Law Review* 2320, 2341–46 (1989).

16. New York Times Co. v. Sullivan, 376 U.S. 254 (1964).

17. It is fascinating that Kalven's treatment of the then one-month-old *Sullivan,* discussing First Amendment issues raised by "the Negro," has not a glimmer of the role of racial politics in the decision. Kalven, *The Negro and the First Amendment.*

18. Brown v. Board of Educ., 349 U.S. 294 (1955). *Brown*'s invalidation of "separate but equal" education was unprincipled, according to Wechsler, because it was a new fact-driven doctrinal leap addressing a problem that was not really about inequality, but about a deprivation of freedom of association. Herbert Wechsler, "Toward Neutral Principles of Constitutional Law," 73 *Harvard Law Review* 1, 31–34 (1959). From a doctrinal perspective, the *Sullivan*

argument that libel could raise First Amendment speech issues was *totally* new. Is libel more obviously speech than segregation is inequality? In the companion case to *Sullivan,* Abernathy v. Sullivan, 376 U.S. at 254, brought against the civil rights leaders themselves, those leaders did complain of the racism and denial of equal protection of aspects of their trial, but not of inequality problems in the speech arguments of the libel claim. *Abernathy* was not chosen by the Supreme Court as the flagship case for its First Amendment decision. For Wechsler's argument in *Sullivan,* see Brief for the Petitioner, New York Times Co. v. Sullivan, 376 U.S. 254 (1964) (No. 39).

19. Sullivan, 376 U.S. at 268–269 (discussing Beauharnais v. Illinois, 343 U.S. 250 (1952)).

20. Dworkin v. Hustler Magazine Inc., 867 F.2d 1188 (9th Cir. 1988), cert. denied, 493 U.S. 812 (1989); Leidholdt v. L.F.P. Inc., 860 F.2d 890 (9th Cir. 1988), cert. denied, 489 U.S. 1080 (1989).

21. Wechsler said in oral argument in *Sullivan* that *Beauharnais* was not correctly decided. 32 U.S.L.W. 3250 (Jan. 14, 1964).

22. Smith v. Collin, 439 U.S. 916 (1978).

23. Kunz v. New York, 340 U.S. 290, 299 (1951) (Jackson, J., dissenting).

24. Usually, they sound in tort. See the creative, audacious, and foundational article by Richard Delgado, "Words That Wound: A Tort Action for Racial Insults, Epithets, and Name-Calling," 17 *Harvard Civil Rights–Civil Liberties Law Review* 133 (1982). Sometimes, in international law or in other countries, hate propaganda laws are rendered as

"antidiscrimination" provisions, but this is little discussed. The major exception, of course, is Canada. See text accompanying note 55 below and Catharine A. MacKinnon, "Pornography as Defamation and Discrimination," 71 *Boston University Law Review* 793, 806 n.33 (1991).

25. Beauharnais, 343 U.S. at 263.
26. Ibid. at 284.
27. Kalven, *The Negro and the First Amendment* at 35.
28. However, in defense of its statute, Illinois did argue that the speech of Beauharnais was unprotected because it led to discrimination in violation of Illinois's state Civil Rights Act. Respondent's Brief, Beauharnais v. Illinois, 343 U.S. 250 (1952) (No. 118) at 4. Such discrimination was argued to be a "substantive evil" that petitioner's publications may "directly tend to incite." Ibid. at 5–6. Illinois also argued that prevention of riots and lynchings is a duty of government and the history of Illinois was "stained with blood spilled from Negroes simply because they were Negroes." Ibid. at 6. "Every riot has its incitement in words." Ibid. Further worth noting, the ACLU argued for Beauharnais that since racial segregation did not violate the federal Civil Rights Act, and "we attorneys for the ACLU have never been so bold to make that invalid suggestion ourselves in our efforts to combat segregation," advocacy of segregation cannot violate the law either. Petitioner's Reply Brief, Beauharnais, 343 U.S. 250 (1952)(No. 118) at 5–6.
29. The most notable victory of this kind is Pittsburgh Press Co. v. Pittsburgh Comm'n on Human Relations, 413 U.S. 376 (1973). Pornography regulation lost in American

Booksellers Ass'n, Inc. v. Hudnut, 771 F.2d 323 (7th Cir. 1985), aff'd, 475 U.S. 1001 (1986). See also State v. Mitchell, 485 N.W.2d 807 (Wis. 1992) (invalidating sentence enhancements on protected grounds under First Amendment), cert. granted, 113 S. Ct. 810 (1992).

30. On campaign financing as speech, see Buckley v. Valeo, 424 U.S. 1 (1976).

31. Cf. Rust v. Sullivan, 111 S. Ct. 1759 (1991).

32. Young v. New York City Transit Authority, 903 F.2d 146 (2d Cir. 1990), cert. denied, 111 S. Ct. 516 (restriction on begging and panhandling in some public transit does not violate First Amendment).

33. Brandenburg v. Ohio, 395 U.S. 444 (1969).

34. NAACP v. Claiborne Hardware Co., 458 U.S. 886 (1982).

35. 42 U.S.C. §2000 (d) et seq. (1988) (Title VI, requiring racial equality in education); 20 U.S.C. §1681 (1988) (Title IX, requiring sex equality in education).

36. Miller, 413 U.S. at 15.

37. Edward DeGrazia appears to support the view that the capacity of a work to produce sexual arousal should be considered a "value" for legal purposes, *Girls Lean Back Everywhere: The Law of Obscenity and the Assault on Genius* 518 (1991).

38. This history, with a different moral to the story, is traced by DeGrazia, ibid. See especially Ginzburg v. United States, 383 U.S. 463, 476 (1966) (Black, J., dissenting) and 482 (Douglas, J., dissenting); Jacobellis v. Ohio, 378 U.S. 184, 196 (1964) (Black, J., concurring); Roth v. United States, 354 U.S. 476, 508 (1957) (Douglas, J., dissenting); Paris

Adult Theatre I v. Slaton, 413 U.S. at 70 (Douglas, J., dissenting) and 73 (Brennan, J., joined by Stewart and Marshall, JJs., dissenting).

39. Kingsley Int'l Pictures Corp. v. Regents of the University of New York, 360 U.S. 684 (1959).

40. The litigation on Deep Throat is a clear example. See citations in Catharine A. MacKinnon, *Feminism Unmodified: Discourses on Life and Law* 34 n.30 (1987).

41. New York v. Ferber, 458 U.S. 747, 762 (1982).

42. Hudnut, 771 F. 2d at 328–329.

43. "... above all else, the First Amendment means that government has no power to restrict expression because of its message [or] ideas..." Ibid. at 328 (quoting Police Department v. Mosley, 408 U.S. at 95). Similar construction of nude dancing as public discourse occurs in the majority opinion in Miller v. Civil City of South Bend, 904 F.2d 1081, 1088 (7th Cir. 1990), invalidating a provision restricting nude dancing. The Supreme Court upheld the provision, reversing the Seventh Circuit in Barnes v. Glen Theatre, Inc., 111 S. Ct. 2456 (1991). See I, pages 31–33.

44. Hudnut, 771 F.2d at 329.

45. Sullivan, 376 U.S. at 270.

46. Hudnut, 771 F.2d at 329.

47. State v. Mitchell, 485 N.W.2d at 820 (Bablitch, J., dissenting). The Supreme Court of Oregon, siding with this dissent, upheld an Oregon hate crime statute against First Amendment attack, Oregon v. Plowman, 838 P.2d 558 (Or. 1992). The U.S. Supreme Court upheld the Wisconsin statute, Wisconsin v. Mitchell, 1993 U.S. LEXIS 4024 (June 11, 1993).

48. Yick Wo v. Hopkins, 118 U.S. 356 (1886).
49. Personnel Administrator v. Feeney, 442 U.S. 256, 272 (1979); Vance v. Bradley, 440 U.S. 93, 97 (1979).
50. This was discussed in I. Schiro v. Clark, 963 F.2d 962 (7th Cir. 1992), cert. granted, May 17, 1993 (No. 92–7549).
51. Schiro, 963 F.2d at 972–973.
52. Arguments of counsel relying on experts Osanka and Donnerstein, Schiro, 963 F.2d at 971–972.
53. The Seventh Circuit affirmed the penalty of death for Schiro on the legally unsatisfying conclusion that although pornographers could be held responsible for some rapes(!), *Hudnut* does not say "the rapist is not also culpable for his own conduct." Schiro, 963 F.2d at 973.
54. Miller, 904 F.2d at 1092 (Posner, J., concurring).
55. Ibid.
56. The Charter came into effect in 1982, the equality provision in 1985.
57. Compare Law Society v. Andrews [1989] 1 S.C.R. 143 (Can.) with Regents of the University of California v. Bakke, 438 U.S. 265 (1978), and City of Richmond v. J. A. Croson Corp., 488 U.S. 469 (1989). The closest the United States has come to approximating the Canadian standard is in California Federal Savings and Loan Ass'n v. Guerra, 479 U.S. 272 (1987), a Title VII case recognizing that legislation to help pregnant women at work promotes sex equality, therefore does not discriminate on the basis of sex.
58. Regina v. Keegstra [1991] 2 W.W.R. 1 (1990) (Can.).
59. Butler v. Regina [1992] 2 W.W.R. 577 (Can.).

60. Ibid. at 594–597, 601, 609.
61. Whitney v. California, 274 U.S. 357, 376 (1927) (Brandeis, J., concurring).
62. This connection was made by Anne E. Simon in a letter to me.
63. First Amendment law has long taken the position that the "sensibilities of readers" must be ignored in deciding whether a state has an interest in suppression of expression. Simon & Schuster, Inc. v. Members of the New York Crime Victims Bd., 112 S. Ct. 501, 509 (1991). As the Court sees it, the offensiveness of an opinion goes to establishing its protection: "The fact that society may find speech offensive is not a sufficient reason for suppressing it. Indeed, if it is the speaker's opinion that gives offense, *that consequence* is a reason for according it constitutional protection." FCC v. Pacifica Foundation, 438 U.S. 726, 745 (1978) (emphasis added), quoted with approval in Hustler Magazine, Inc. v. Falwell, 485 U.S. 46, 55 (1988). See also Texas v. Johnson, 491 U.S. 397, 414 (1989): "If there is a bedrock principle underlying the First Amendment, it is that the Government may not prohibit the expression of an idea simply because society finds the idea itself offensive or disagreeable." These authorities were found to support the view in *Simon & Schuster* that the Crime Board "does not assert any interest in limiting whatever anguish Henry Hill's victims may suffer from reliving their victimization," 112 S. Ct. at 509. *Hudnut* states that the role of pornography in perpetuating subordination "simply demonstrates the power of pornography as speech." 771 F.2d at 329. As distinguished from *Hudnut,* in *Simon & Schuster* it was not

asserted that the crimes were committed to produce the accounts of the crimes, as women coerced into pornography assert; nor does *Simon & Schuster* bar civil recovery for damages either for mental anguish or to reputational or privacy interests. There was also no claim in that case that the portrayals of the crime victims were false, defamatory, placed them in a false light, or discriminated against them.

64. Roberts v. U.S. Jaycees, 468 U.S. 609, 623 (1984), holds that states have a "compelling interest in eradicating discrimination" on the basis of sex, which can outweigh the First Amendment right of association, as it did here. In ruling against the First Amendment challenge, and in favor of statutory sex equality, *Roberts* states that "acts of invidious discrimination in the distribution of goods, services, and other advantages cause unique evils that government has a compelling interest to prevent—wholly apart from the point of view such conduct may transmit... Accordingly... such practices are entitled to no constitutional protection." Ibid. at 628.

65. Thomas I. Emerson, *The System of Freedom of Expression* 496 (1970): "A communication of this [erotic] nature, imposed upon a person contrary to his wishes, has all the characteristics of a physical assault" and "can therefore realistically be classified as action." A comparison with his preliminary formulation in *Toward a General Theory of the First Amendment* 91 (1963) suggests that his view on this subject became stronger by his 1970 revisiting of the issue.

INDEX

Murder *(cont.)*
  bigoted incitement to, 34,
  124n54; obscenity law and, 91;
  pornography affecting mental
  state of murderer, 95–96; in
  cults, 120n28; liability of publisher for as result of published
  ad, 120n30

*NAACP v. Claiborne Hardware
  Co.,* 86, 142n34
Nazis' march in Skokie, Illinois,
  82–83, 105, 106
New York Times Co. v. Sullivan,
  78–82, 93, 139nn16, 18, 19, 21,
  143n45
New York v. Ferber, 122n34,
  143n41; Brief of American
  Booksellers Ass'n et al. in,
  125nn56, 57
NLRB v. Gissel Packing Co.,
  132n36
Norberg v. Wynrib, 113n1
Norville, Deborah, 66
Nude dancing, 31–33, 85, 97,
  123nn42, 44, 143n43

Obscenity, 8–9, 23; pervasiveness
  of, 51; "deprave and corrupt the
  morals of consumers" test for,
  87; historical background of law,
  87; ineffectuality of obscenity
  law, 87–89, 90–91; "prurient interest" test for, 88; violation of
  community standards test for,
  88, 101; harm outweighing value
  test for, 91; Indianapolis ordinance, 91–94, 96, 107, 121n32;
  Canadian law, 100–102, 103; expression of offensive ideas as,
  138n13. *See also* Censorship;
  Speech

*Olivia N. v. National Broadcasting
  Co.,* 122n37
Oregon v. Plowman, 143n47
Organized crime, 20, 120n28
Osborne v. Ohio, 122n35, 125n58

Palmer v. Thompson, 116n16
Paris Adult Theatre I v. Slaton,
  139n13, 142n38
Penthouse magazine, 36, 37
People v. Burnham, 113n1
Personnel Administrator v. Feeney,
  123n40, 144n49
Pierson v. Ray, 117n16
*Pittsburgh Press Co. v. Pittsburgh
  Comm'n on Human Relations,*
  117n18, 140n29
Playboy magazine, 22–23
Police Department v. Mosley,
  136n2, 143n43
Pornography: and subordination
  of women, 10, 20–23, 24–27, 29,
  58–60, 68, 88, 90, 92, 100–102;
  defined, 22–23, 24; as fantasy,
  26; "simulation" in, 27–29;
  meaning of for women, 29–31;
  Model Ordinance definition,
  121n32
Posner, Judge Richard A., 10, 97
Prostitution, 24, 28, 85; nude
  dancing and, 32; obscenity law
  and, 91

Rabidue v. Osceola Refining Co.,
  128n5, 130nn24, 26, 27, 132n37
Race discrimination. *See* Discrimination
Racial harassment, 49–50, 51, 52,
  61; in education, 53–54, 55; race
  and sex analogy, 55–58
Racism, 62, 74, 80; sexualization
  of, 23, 45, 57–58, 60, 63–64, 66;